SECRET
WASHINGTON, DC

A Guide to the Weird, Wonderful, and Obscure

JoAnn Hill

Reedy Press
PO Box 5131
St. Louis, MO 63139
www.reedypress.com

Library of Congress Control Number: 2020950057
ISBN: 9781681063096

Design by Jill Halpin

Printed in the United States of America
22 23 24 25   5 4 3 2

To Thalamus:
My greatest love, my strongest champion, and my biggest supporter.
I love you a lot a lot.

CONTENTS

ACKNOWLEDGMENTS

They say it takes a village, and perhaps no other undertaking in my life has embodied this adage more. I am deeply indebted to the many individuals and organizations that have generously shared their time, insight, and resources to help make this project possible. There were those who graciously welcomed me into their homes to not only share their incredible art and collections, but also to share their remarkable stories. To perhaps the most interesting man alive, Hoff the Harmonica Case Man, and home design extraordinaires Andrea Peterson and Matt Separa, thank you. There were others who were exceedingly generous with their time, meeting me over coffee and speaking with me on the phone: to musician Jason Mendelson, artists Mark Cline, Clarke Bedford, and Howard Connelly, and history-buffs Tim Krepp and Tamara Belden, thank you. To Julie Marshall of Washington.org, who tirelessly assisted me with procuring photos and connecting me with other agencies, thank you. To the knowledgeable tour guides, park rangers, and museum curators who kindly shared fascinating stories and tidbits and were more than eager to help with this project, thank you.

To the wonderful team at Reedy Press, especially Josh Stevens, thank you for your guidance, collaboration, and expertise.

When an opportunity arises and practically falls into your lap, you embrace it and say yes. Thank you, Christine Ruiz, for extending this extraordinary opportunity and helping make this pipe dream a reality.

To my mom and dad, for their perpetual sacrifice and instilling the values of hard work and tenacity, thank you.

And to my biggest supporter and best friend, my husband Thalamus, thank you. There has never been a moment that you haven't been right by my side cheering me on every step of the way. Thank you for being the best person I know and for making me want to be the best version of myself. I love you so very much.

INTRODUCTION

Around the world, Washington, DC, is known for its powerful government, majestic monuments, and world-renowned museums. While my research inevitably led me to these popular points of interest, once I began to delve below the surface, my attention and interest immediately shifted to the off-the-grid locales, the eccentric individuals, and the hidden histories that have helped shape the city I have called home for over 19 years. *Secret Washington, DC* reminds us that the fabric of the city isn't solely embedded into its callous political parties, exhausting lawmaking policies, and rampant tourism. Rather, it's woven through its rich and complex history, mysterious relics and underground societies, forgotten and abandoned institutions, and controversial and often unknown scandals. From carefully executed assassinations, to crimes of passion and accidental shootings, to signs of hope and innovation, *Secret Washington, DC* uncovers many of the untold truths of how our nation emerged and continues to flourish.

Here you'll discover subterranean catacombs, a carousel linked to the Civil Rights Movement, a captivating collection of Barbie dolls serving as political activists, and a miraculous bonsai tree that managed to survive the bombing of Hiroshima. You'll explore lesser-known memorials honoring musicians and women, while learning shocking facts about the ones you thought you already knew. You'll acquaint yourself with brilliant artists who have made masterpieces out of furniture, tin foil, and foam. You'll explore homes ranging from the mushroom-inspired to the penny-centric to the narrowest and smallest there is. You'll learn where you can propose like a president, follow in the footsteps of cunning spies, stop along a roadside pit-stop to pray, and sing along to metro-inspired tunes while riding the longest single-span escalator in the western hemisphere.

From quirky oddities, to enchanted forests, to bizarre burial sites, to signs of the occult, *Secret Washington, DC* will introduce you to the other side of Washington, DC: a treasure trove of mystique, peculiarities, and hidden history just waiting to be explored.

JEFFERSON MEMORIAL: LEAVE THOSE DANCING SHOES AT HOME

What is quite possibly the strangest and most surprising law that has emerged out of our nation's capital?

There may be a time and place to dance like no one's watching, but dance enthusiasts should beware of adding the Jefferson Memorial to their lists of dance venues.

On May 17, 2011, a federal appeals court in Washington, DC declared expressive dancing as prohibited inside the Jefferson Memorial. The US Court of Appeals for the DC Circuit stated that expressive dancing "falls into the spectrum" of prohibited activities, including picketing, demonstrations, and speechmaking, at the memorial. The rules are intended to ban conduct that has the propensity to attract spectators while detracting from the dignified and ceremonious setting of the national memorial.

The court's ruling was in response to the 2008 arrest of Mary Brooke Oberwetter, along with other dancers, for silently dancing to commemorate Thomas Jefferson's 265th birthday. The dancers' expressive dance performance was deemed as unlawful. While Oberwetter argued that the federal regulations that govern the use of the memorial do not prohibit silent dance, the court still viewed the performance as a

THE JEFFERSON MEMORIAL

WHAT: A national memorial honoring the United States' third president, Thomas Jefferson

WHERE: 16 E. Basin Drive SW, Washington, DC

COST: Free

PRO TIP: The Jefferson Memorial is open 24 hours a day, every day of the year. Rangers are on duty from 9:30 a.m. to 10 p.m. daily.

Top: *Jefferson Memorial illuminated at night. Photo courtesy of Washington.org.*
Inset: *Statue of Thomas Jefferson standing tall inside his memorial. Photo courtesy of Washington.org.*

distraction to fellow visitors, as well as an attraction to onlookers.

While some of the laws passed in our nation's capital have caused many to scratch their heads, this one may just be among the strangest and surprising of them all.

Franklin Roosevelt insisted that the location of the Jefferson Memorial have a clear view of the White House. Because of its location on the Tidal Basin where the famous cherry blossoms are planted, construction workers were forced to remove some trees.

DISCORD AND DISCOLORATION AT THE US CAPITOL

Why are the US Capitol's marble stairs discolored by the stain of human blood?

While discord between politicians and the media seems to frequently inundate today's headlines, tension between the two is nothing new. In fact, dissonance between lawmakers and the media dates back to the early history of our nation.

On February 28, 1890, Charles Kincaid, a newspaper correspondent for the Louisville Times, fatally shot former Congressman William Taulbee of Kentucky. The two men had had a tumultuous history since 1887 when Kincaid wrote a story accusing Taulbee of an extramarital affair.

The congressman chose not to run for a third term; however, his work as a lobbyist kept the two closely connected. Throughout their three-year relationship, Kincaid and Taulbee exchanged numerous verbal insults. On the day of the shooting, House doorkeepers had to separate the two men. Taulbee reportedly warned the reporter to arm himself. Kincaid later met up with Taulbee and fatally shot him on the east staircase of the House Wing of the Capitol. The media widely covered the egregious event. Kincaid was later acquitted by a jury, citing self-defense.

The permanent discoloration from Taulbee's blood is still evident on the marble stairs leading to the White House Press

---

The blood-stained steps continue to be a reminder to some superstitious journalists who choose to cautiously walk to the side of the stained droplets in hopes of avoiding an unfortunate fate.

The exterior of US Capitol's Visitor's Center illuminated at night. Photo courtesy of the Architect of the Capitol.

Gallery and marks the location of the shocking shooting. While freedom of the press and public discourse is vital to any thriving nation, this tragic exchange serves as a harsh reminder that it is not without its challenges and downfalls.

THE US CAPTIOL

WHAT: Home of the United States Congress and the seat of the legislative branch of the US federal government

WHERE: First Street SE, Washington, DC

COST: Free

PRO TIP: Free tours are offered to the public and advance reservations are recommended.

STAIRWAY TO CREEPINESS

Where can movie buffs and fitness fanatics find the creepiest staircase in all of DC?

The historic neighborhood of Georgetown boasts a prestigious university, expensive real estate, a plethora of high-end retail shops and boutiques, and a bevy of convivial eateries and watering holes. That's not all, however. This quaint neighborhood has also added a super frightening staircase to its already impressive resume.

Near the now-closed Exxon Mobil station, where M Street becomes Canal Road, passersby will notice an extremely long, steep staircase nestled between a stone wall and a brick warehouse.

Fans of the 1973 horror movie *The Exorcist* may recognize the stairs as the site of the dramatic final exchange between the self-sacrificing priest and the demon who possesses twelve-year-old Regan. The staircase's narrow dimensions and ivy-draped walls add to its mystique and eeriness.

While some may find themselves intimidated by the arduous climb, the inherently creepy stairs also serve as a shortcut between Prospect Street NW above and Canal Road NW below. Climbers who make their way up the 97 steps to the top will be rewarded by the site of the actual home from the movie located to the left at 3600 Prospect Street MW.

Decades after its release, the *Exorcist* stairs continue to thrill both devout movie buffs and exercise enthusiasts.

THE EXORCIST STAIRS

WHAT: Site of the staircase featured in the iconic horror film *The Exorcist*

WHERE: 36th and M Streets NW, Georgetown, Washington, DC

COST: Free

PRO TIP: Drive east along M Street. Just before it turns into Canal St. NW, you will see Exxon Mobil on the right. You will be at the bottom of the stairs.

Above: Exorcist *Stairs in Georgetown. Photo courtesy of Sarah Stierch.* Inset: *Row homes of Georgetown. Photo courtesy of Washington.org.*

While Regan's room built for the movie is no longer connected, it still remains part of the property just behind a black gate.

I GOT YOU, BABE

What's the story behind the compact memorial dedicated to late singer Sonny Bono?

Think every national memorial needs to be majestic, made of marble or stone, and teeming with tourists? Think again. Some memorials are tiny, tranquil, and quite easy to miss if you don't know where and what you're looking for.

In 1998, long-time DC resident and real estate developer Geary Simon dedicated an 800-square-foot triangular patch of grass as a memorial to late legendary singer Salvatore Bono, known to millions around the world as Sonny Bono.

While Bono is mostly known for his work as a recording artist and former husband of music icon Cher, he also served as a representative for California's 44th District, holding this office until his fatal ski accident in 1998. It was during Bono's time in office that he and Simon met and became close friends.

Following Bono's shocking death, Simon contacted the DC Department of Parks and Recreation and took advantage of DC's Adopt-a-Park program to convert an overgrown and unkept traffic triangle near Dupont Circle into an urban shrine commemorating his dear friend.

Simon contributed tens of thousands of dollars of his own money and was the leading force behind the memorial's design. While the renovated park was a significant upgrade to the formerly abandoned and rat-infested lot, in the beginning it was not welcomed by all of its neighbors. Some argued that a piece of city land should not be arbitrarily used to memorialize whomever a

---

A small bronze plaque fondly reads, In Memory of My Friend Sonny Bono 1935–1998, with the words Entertainer, Entrepreneur, Statesman, Friend surrounding the inscription.

Sonny Bono Memorial Park: Commemorating a friend and musical legend. Photos courtesy of JoAnn Hill.

SONNY BONO MEMORIAL PARK

WHAT: A small park in Northwest DC honoring late singer and representative Sonny Bono

WHERE: At the intersection of New Hampshire Avenue, 20th Street, and O Street near Dupont Circle, Washington, DC

COST: Free

PRO TIP: The park is less than a five-minute walk from Dupont Circle metro station.

private citizen deemed worthy. Despite some opposition, plans for the memorial park were carried to completion.

Sonny Bono Memorial Park features underground lights, stone benches, imported Kentucky bluegrass, and a tree from Bono's congressional district in Southern California. The peaceful park is a loving reminder that DC's got you, Sonny. Today and always.

NAME THAT TUNE: THE METRO EDITION

How can one person's commuter nightmare be someone else's creative muse?

Doors closing and all of those endless chimes. Just a few words and sounds often associated with DC's Metrorail system, the second busiest metro system in the United States. What most people don't realize, however, is that these words and sounds don't even begin to scratch the surface of this metro rail system that is laden with history. Thanks to local musician Jason Mendelson, there is now a lyrical song that corresponds to each and every one of Washington's 91 Metrorail system's stations.

In April of 2017, Mendelson finished writing his 91st song, completing eight albums in total. Mendelson devoted 6 ½ years of his life to this ambitious project, aptly named MetroSongs. He collaborated with more than 20 different musicians and groups on this project. A native of Tampa, Florida, Mendelson grew up in an area where public transportation wasn't readily available. DC's extensive 118-mile rail system offered him a relatively easy and efficient way to become acquainted with the metropolis. His appreciation for DC's rail system, along with his creativity, helped propel his musical career throughout the Washington metro area. Known to some as "The Metro Guy," Mendelson soon found himself

---

91 METRO STATION SONGS

WHAT: Songs written for each of DC's 91 metro stations, spanning 8 albums

WHERE: Metro stations, as well as Mendelson's gigs, can be found throughout the DC metro area.

COST: Volumes 3–8 can be streamed on Spotify/Apple/YouTube or wherever streaming is available, as well as on Bandcamp.

PRO TIP: Mendelson performs at various music venues around the DC area including the Electric Maid, IOTA, the Kennedy Center, and 9:30 Club.

Top: *Smithsonian metro station: One of 91 metro stations songs featured on Jason Mendelson's Metro Album Collection. Photo courtesy of Washington.org.* Inset: *DC area songwriter and singer Jason Mendelson. Photo courtesy of Jason Mendelson.*

booked at various music venues throughout the metro DC area.

Mendelson's 91 tracks cover a wide array of topics. Some convey a unique story about its neighborhood's history. "Congress Heights," for example, recounts the history of St. Elizabeths Hospital, the country's first federally run psychiatric facility. Others focus on global issues and interests. "Anacostia" focuses on the Black Lives Matter movement, while "Vienna" details espionage. MetroSongs makes it easy for Washingtonians to connect to the neighborhoods surrounding Metrorail stations in a fun and informative way.

It also proves that sometimes even the most surprising and mundane places can serve as a creative muse.

Mendelson brings an enormous "Wheel of Metro" to his shows. The wheel features station names, and audience members can spin it to determine what songs Mendelson and his band play.

ONE MAN'S TRASH IS ANOTHER MAN'S MASTERPIECE

How can a heap of junk be transformed into an artistic masterpiece?

As the old adage goes: One man's trash is another man's treasure. James Hampton, Director of Special Projects for the State of Eternity, took that timeless sentiment to heart, proving that many everyday discarded items can actually be converted into stunning objects of art.

After receiving religious visions, Hampton devoted over 14 years of his life to constructing a monument to God, eventually known around the world as The Throne of the Third Heaven of the Nations' Millennium General Assembly, which is prominently displayed in The Smithsonian's American Art Museum.

In 1950, Hampton undertook this elaborate project in hopes of preparing for Christ's return to earth. He created his grand showpiece in a rented carriage house, transforming its dull interior into a magnificent workspace. He assembled coffee cans, jelly jars, flower vases, lightbulbs, metal, scrap wood, plastic, and tinfoil into something magical. He also incorporated old furniture and various office supplies into the brilliant structure. The Throne is comprised of two levels. A cushioned throne in the back is a central point for the extremely symmetrical array. Objects on the right represent the New Testament and Jesus; those on the left portray the Old Testament and Moses. The Throne is constructed from 177 pieces

The Throne of Third Heaven is so beloved in the art world that when the museum was reopened after renovations in 2006, the Smithsonian chose The Throne as its first piece to be reinstalled.

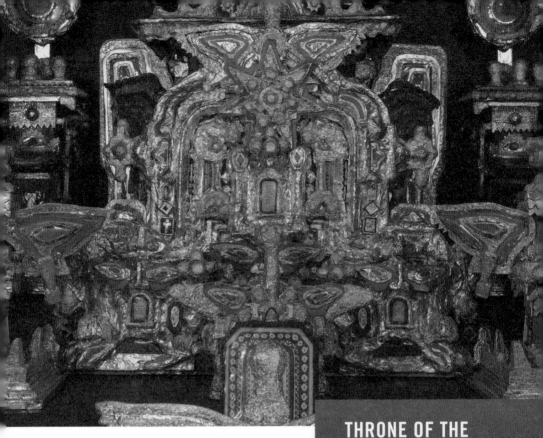

The intricate and elaborate Throne of the Third Heaven of the Nations' Millennium General Assembly at the Smithsonian American Art Museum. Photo courtesy of James Hampton.

THRONE OF THE THIRD HEAVEN

WHAT: James Hampton's art masterpiece, a monument to God, constructed of various recycled materials

WHERE: Smithsonian American Art Museum: 8th & F Streets NW, Washington, DC

COST: Free

PRO TIP: The museum is open every day 11:30 a.m. to 7:00 p.m.

in all, spanning nearly 200 square feet, and stands nine feet tall at its center.

Since Hampton chose to work privately, it was only after his death in 1964 that his work was shared with the art world. No one knew of Hampton's creation except for his landlord, who took possession of it all in exchange of back rent. The Throne has been widely recognized as America's greatest visionary work of art. James Hampton was indeed ahead of his time, recognizing the unparalleled value and effectiveness of recycling.

J, JAY, OR I: THE REAL REASON WHY THERE IS NO J STREET

What does Washington, DC, have against the letter J?

Ask even the most astute Washingtonian why J Street has been excluded from the District's streets, and chances are you will receive

a wide array of answers. In a city where the letters of the alphabet dominate addresses and points of interest, the letter J's omission is as noticeable as it is mythologized.

DC designer Pierre L'Enfant methodically planned the city on a grid, with number streets running North–South, letter streets running East–West, and streets named after states running on diagonal streets. So why did L'Enfant intentionally leave J Street off of his design plan?

The most popular (albeit, incorrect) theory is that J Street was purposely left off of the map because L'Enfant despised John Jay, the new nation's first Supreme Court Chief Justice. The two men were often at odds as a result of belonging to rival political parties. While their rivalry may be riveting to some, it is not the reason why J Street does not exist.

Both Washingtonians and tourists can blame the Latin language for the omission of J Street. In the English alphabet, which is based on the Latin alphabet, the letter J looked too much like the letter I.

Busy intersection of Wisconsin Avenue and M Street in Georgetown. Photo courtesy of Washington.org.

There is no letter J in Latin. At times during the Middle Ages, a J would be used as a substitute for the final I in Roman numerals (e.g., iij for 3 instead of iii). In hopes of avoiding any confusion, the letter J was intentionally left off of the city grid.

So, while the real story for the lack of a J Street may not be as scandalous as some other aspects of our nation's capital, some may find consolation that a Jay Street does exist in Northeast DC.

In order to avoid the same letter confusion, there is no J Company in a US Army battalion.

A FAIRYLAND TO CALL HOME

Where in the DC area can you live in a complex that looks like it's straight out of Disney's Epcot?

Those looking to venture a few miles outside of Washington, DC, may find themselves transported into a magical, albeit bizarre land. Part whimsical fairytale and part residential community, the National Park Seminary at Forest Glen somehow manages to beautifully tie the two unlikely concepts together.

The National Park Seminary has undergone a number of changes since it was established in 1887. The property began as a tobacco plantation before turning into Ye Forest Inn, a high-end tourist resort for affluent Washingtonians. In 1894, the buildings were converted into an all-girls' finishing school called the National Park Seminary. The elaborate, meticulously designed architecture on campus was based on plans from the Chicago World's Fair. The girls lived in eight unusually constructed sorority houses; each model represented a different country's architecture style. One was modeled on a Japanese pagoda, another on a Dutch windmill, and another on a Swiss chalet. This unique design earned acclaim across the region, attracting some of the time's wealthiest families, including the Hersheys, Krafts, Chryslers, and Maytags. After thriving for several decades, the seminary faced a number of setbacks, and during World War II it was taken over by the US Army, which used the campus to house recovering amputees, and later wounded soldiers, during the Vietnam and Korean wars.

Even though the seminary was placed on the National Register of Historic Places in 1972, by 1978 it had been neglected for far too long and fell into disrepair. Thanks to the Save Our Seminary

---

The National Park Seminary also boasts a resplendent ballroom complete with vaulted ceilings and oak finishes, as well as a vine-covered English castle with a drawbridge.

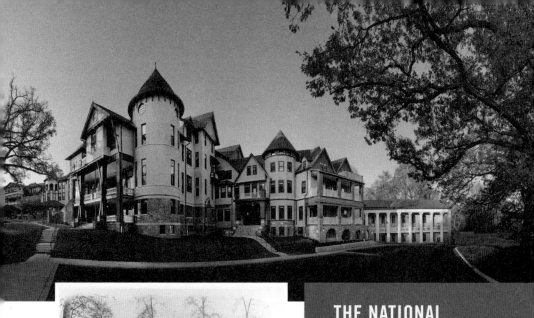

The National Park Seminary exterior complex. Photos courtesy of Alexander Company.

THE NATIONAL PARK SEMINARY AT FOREST GLEN

WHAT: A present-day fairytale-like residential community that was once a plantation, girls' finishing school, and Army-run soldier hospital

WHERE: 9615 Dewitt Dr., Silver Spring, MD

COST: Free

PRO TIP: Save Our Seminary offers public guided tours from March through November on the fourth Saturday of the month. Private tours can be arranged for $5 per person.

association, it was saved from demolition. By 2003, a developer had taken over the complex and revived it as a residential community, with the historic buildings transformed into houses and condos. Today, there are over 200 apartments, condos, and town homes available for rent or purchase. Six of the eight original sorority houses have been re-energized into residences, including the Dutch windmill and Japanese pagoda.

FIRST LADY SÉANCE AT THE SOLDIERS' HOME

Why did Mary Todd Lincoln frequently attend séances?

Today President Lincoln's Cottage, a national monument situated on the grounds of the Soldiers' Home, is the esteemed setting of the Armed Forces Retirement Home. In the 1800s, however, the Soldiers' Home served as a meeting place for spirit circles, known as séances, where bereaved individuals would gather to communicate with deceased loved ones. Perhaps the most recognized attendees were Mary Todd Lincoln and her husband, President Abraham Lincoln.

After the death of their son Willie in 1862, a grieving Mary Lincoln began to attend these séances, where a medium would help those gathered communicate with lost loved ones. Spirits communicated in various ways, including scratching, rapping, playing instruments, pulling on clothing or hair, and pinching participants. While there were many skeptics, spiritualism appealed to many, regardless of class, particularly following the heavy death toll during the Civil War.

Despite increased popularity of séances, Mrs. Lincoln's involvement attracted gossip and condemnation, not just of

Left: *President Lincoln's Cottage: A national monument and historical home.* Right: *A look inside Lincoln's Cottage. Photos courtesy of Carol M. Highsmith.*

her, but of Abraham Lincoln, who periodically joined her. Historians maintain Lincoln frequented séances out of curiosity or support for his wife, not out of credence. President Lincoln was dubious of mediums, particularly of one named Lord Colchester, a man who claimed to be the illegitimate son of an English duke. Lincoln summoned Dr. Joseph Henry, first Secretary of the Smithsonian, to look into the questionable medium. When Henry was unable to identify the origin of the spirit rappings Colchester called forth, he asked Noah Brooks, a journalist and friend of Lincoln's, to investigate a séance at the Soldiers' Home. Brooks deduced that Colchester, not spirits, was responsible for making "music in the air" and was indeed a fraud. Colchester later tried to blackmail Mary Lincoln, but Brooks interceded, helping to avert any potential scandal or further denunciation. Undeterred, Mary Lincoln continued to participate in spirit circles throughout her life, communicating with sons Willie and Eddie as well as other deceased relatives.

According to Earl Schenck Miers's *Lincoln: Day by Day*, President Lincoln allegedly attended the séance at the Soldiers' Home on April 23, 1863. While séances also occurred at the White House, there is no record of Lincoln being there.

TAKING A STAND

Where did the National Arboretum's dramatic Corinthian columns come from?

One of the most distinctive and imposing installations of the National Arboretum is undoubtedly the National Capitol Columns. Standing on an expansive grassy knoll, the 22 soaring Corinthian columns piercing the looming sky produce a dramatic and striking scene. Their utter dominance of the space creates the illusion that they've been a permanent fixture of the arboretum since its opening in 1927, when, in fact, they're actually a somewhat recent addition.

The notable columns originally supported the east portico of the US Capitol in 1828. They had been quarried from sandstone in Virginia and then transported by freight to Washington before the current Capitol dome was completed. When the iron dome was finally completed in 1864, nearly four decades after the completion of the columns, the architects realized they had made a mistake in their plans. The columns were unable to properly support the new dome because it was significantly larger than initially intended. There was a proposal to build an addition to the Capitol's east side in hopes of rectifying the lopsided appearance, but it wasn't constructed until 1958. After nearly a century had passed, it seemed like the Grecian-styled columns were all but forgotten.

It wasn't until 1984 that the famed columns moved to their final and forever home. National Arboretum benefactress Ethel Garrett and other private donors worked together to retrieve the pristine columns out of storage and under the US government's

---

The columns stand on a foundation that was once steps also located on the east side of the US Capitol. Marks from the Virginia quarry are still visible on some of the stones.

The National Arboretum's 22 Corinthian columns: one of DC's most distinguishable landmarks. Photo courtesy of washington.org

ownership of the arboretum. Russell Page, a friend of Garrett's and a landscape artist, established the ideal setting for the ornate columns, on the east side of the Ellipse, allowing the majestic columns to be proportionate with the 20-plus acres of open field.

NATIONAL CAPITOL COLUMNS

WHAT: Twenty-two Corinthian columns that were once part of the US Capitol and now grace the National Arboretum's expansive meadow

WHERE: The National Arboretum: 3501 New York Ave. NE, Washington, DC

COST: Free

PRO TIP: The National Capitol Columns is open every day of the year (except December 25th) from 8 a.m. to 5 p.m.

ABUSED AND ABANDONED: THE DEMISE OF THE FOREST HAVEN ASYLUM

How did a once-progressive psychiatric facility become infamous for rampant abuse and maltreatment?

Approximately 20 miles outside of DC in Laurel, Maryland, sits a dilapidated and abandoned compound that once harbored thousands of the city's most mentally disabled residents. The expansive 200-acre, 22-building complex has a sordid past filled with maltreatment and abuse.

The Forest Haven Asylum opened in 1925 as a progressive mental health institution. It was a farm colony that taught everyday skills to mentally disabled individuals with the goal of getting them employed. Residents milked cows, planted and took care of crops, and lived in dormitories surrounded by greenery as well as basketball courts and athletic fields. Their daily schedule included exercise and leisure. Over time, however, the level of care began to deteriorate, and funding ran out. Recreation and athletic programs were eventually cut, primarily affecting residents who weren't actually mentally disabled, but either severely epileptic or otherwise disabled to the point that they struggled to function outside of the asylum. Many who were once mobile languished due to inactivity, ultimately becoming bedridden. To further compound issues, the institution became overcrowded and

FOREST HAVEN ASYLUM

WHAT: An abandoned psychiatric hospital where patients were severely mistreated and many died

WHERE: Right off of Route 197 in Fort Meade, MD

COST: Free for those brave enough to visit

PRO TIP: Entrance is prohibited by the police.

The abandoned and decrepit Forest Haven Asylum. Photo courtesy of Will Fisher.

operated by underqualified staff members; some of the doctors were even determined medically incompetent by the state of Maryland. Pervasive abuse of every kind—physical, sexual, mental—was widely reported.

Even more alarming were the staggering number of deaths reported. Hundreds of bodies were transported down to a cramped basement morgue and entombed in an unmarked grave on the asylum grounds. Numerous families purchased a single headstone that serves as a memorial to the 387 individuals buried beneath it. In 1976, families filed a class-action lawsuit, citing the countless abuses at the facility. The District had no choice but to respond. In 1978, the first step in rebuilding its flailing mental health system was taken when residents were relocated to other locations including group homes and other health facilities.

Various items including deteriorated dentist chairs, old-school Pepsi machines, tattered medical journals, and old patient files can still be found at the Forest Haven Asylum.

BUILT ON A BORDELLO AND THE OLDEST PROFESSION IN THE WORLD

What lies beneath The National Museum of the American Indian?

Throughout history, entrepreneurship has been a hard-fought battle for countless women around the world. While successful businesswomen are certainly more common in today's workplace, in the 1800s, they were exceedingly rare. Meet Mary Ann Hall: the 20-something woman who built and ran the largest and most exclusive of more than 100 bordellos in Washington during the 1800s.

Hall's three-story establishment, situated on the grassy expanse of land that now houses the Smithsonian's National Museum of the American Indian, thrived for more than 40 years. The astute businesswoman selected the location of her brothel because it was convenient to Capitol Hill, a prime location because of the large number of visiting businessmen who typically traveled and arrived alone.

The onset of the Civil War in 1861 brought a new batch of men to Washington, including thousands of soldiers, civil servants, freed and escaped slaves, businessmen, and swindlers, as well as prostitutes looking for work. By 1864, Hall's high-end operation was booming, employing more prostitutes than any other brothel in the city, and soon became the most expensive piece of real estate

---

Some of the remains discovered from the brothel include broken porcelain dishes, seeds, animal bones, ceramic tableware, and Champagne bottles and corks. Further examination of the relics suggests residents of the brothel lived much more extravagantly than the average person in other nearby neighborhoods.

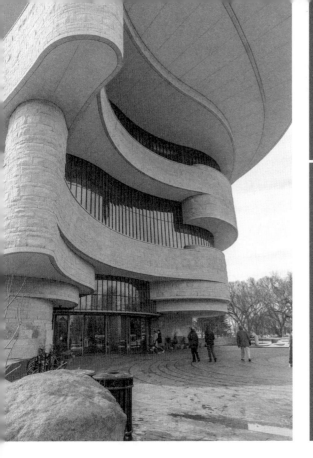

WHAT: The National Museum of the American Indian stands on the site where Mary Ann Hall once operated a highly prosperous brothel

WHERE: Independence Avenue SW, Washington, DC

COST: Free

PRO TIP: The nearest metro station is the Federal Center SW metro station on the Blue and Orange Lines.

The architectural wonder of the National Museum of the American Indian. Photo courtesy of Washington.org.

in the neighborhood. As the war concluded, the region between Pennsylvania Avenue and the Mall, presently identified as the Federal Triangle district, became widely referred to as Hooker's Division, due to its pervasive prostitution and crime-infested streets. Around the same time, the area encompassing Hall's house and similar operations formed a compact red-light district.

Hall continued to operate her prosperous bordello into the 1870s before retiring as a madam. In 1883, she rented out part of the building to the Washington Dispensary, which opened up a women's health clinic.

Over a century later, a law was signed authorizing the building of the National Museum of the American Indian on top of the former brothel. An excavation on the museum site revealed the remnants of the bordello and various artifacts buried below the foundation.

HUDDLE UP: A SIGN OF THE TIMES

At which esteemed Washington, DC, university was the American football huddle invented?

American football has been a favorite pastime across the country for decades. For well over a century, fans have watched their favorite teams gather on the field in huddles, strategizing and calling out plays and game plans. But where did the idea of the modern football huddle come from?

In 1892, Paul Hubbard, a quarterback who played for Gallaudet University (the largest deaf and hard-of-hearing university in the world, located in Northeast DC) called for his offense to circle up so that the opposing team couldn't see the plays they were signing. Hubbard served as Gallaudet's quarterback from 1892 to 1895 and used the huddle as a means of keeping his signed play calling secret from any opposing player who may have known sign language.

The idea of the huddle, however, took some time to catch on. In fact, various college fans throughout the country complained that the huddle slowed down the game. It took nearly 30 years for one of the first

ORIGIN OF THE AMERICAN FOOTBALL HUDDLE AT GALLAUDET UNIVERSITY

WHAT: The modern American football huddle was first used by Paul Hubbard, a quarterback who played for Gallaudet University, the world's largest deaf and hard-of-hearing university

WHERE: 800 Florida Ave. NE, Washington, DC

COST: Tickets to Gallaudet footballs games are general admission; $10 per ticket

PRO TIP: Before Gallaudet University became a world-renowned institution for the advanced education for the deaf and hard-of-hearing, it was a grammar school for both deaf and blind children.

Top: *Gallaudet Bison football team getting ready to play ball. Photo courtesy of David Fulmer.* Inset: *Gallaudet University: geared to the deaf and hard of hearing. Photo courtesy of Andrew Kuchling.*

major universities to use a huddle in a game. In 1918, the Oregon Agriculture College, now known as the Oregon State Beavers, used a version of the huddle, where players stood 10 yards behind the line of scrimmage for players to discuss their next play.

Although Gallaudet is credited with originating the huddle, the team eventually did away with it, opting to sign their plays out in the open, since the teams they play against don't typically know sign language. While Gallaudet no longer employs the huddle, it has proven to be a permanent and integral fixture in professional and amateur football games around the world.

Gallaudet was founded in 1864, and in 1887 the university began accepting women into their university.

MICRO SHOWCASE & FIVE SIGNS: SMALL SIZES, BIG REGRETS

Where in Washington, DC, is minimalism, sustainability, and off-the-grid living proudly showcased?

In a city greatly defined by its pervasive magnitude—colossal monuments, grand museums, and big government—it's nice to know that not all things in our nation's capital are built on a grandiose scale. Welcome to the Micro Showcase, a tucked-away display of microstructures that promotes sustainability, minimalism, and off-the-grid living.

Hidden in a small alleyway across from Glenwood Cemetery are a number of skillfully constructed mini buildings and homes, all under 350 square feet. The micro concept is intended to promote the importance and ability to live "small," focusing on sustainable technologies including off-grid solar, rain-capture and treatment, and micro furnishings. The Showcase project emphasizes that oversized US housing is detrimental to our environment, contributing 20% to US CO_2 emissions.

To add to the alleyway's intrigue, mounted on the fence surrounding the micro community is an exhibit that has been titled "Five Regrets of the Dying," an installation of five green and white signs that portray common themes and repentance among the dying. Broonie Ware, an Australian nurse who spent several years working in palliative care, documented her patients' greatest regrets during the final 12 weeks of their lives. Two of the five regrets

---

The "Five Regrets of Dying" signs installation and Micro Showcase are tucked away around the corner on a quiet street next to the Glenwood Cemetery.

Top: *Living small and purposeful: The tiny homes that make up the Micro Showcase complex.* Inset: *Inside one of the complex's micro homes. Photos courtesy of Minim Homes LLC.*

MICRO SHOWCASE AND FIVE REGRETS

WHAT: A display of micro buildings and homes, all under 350 square feet. The "Five Regrets" is a collection of signs portraying five common themes and regrets among the dying

WHERE: 21 Evarts St. NE, Washington, DC

COST: Free

PRO TIP: Walking north on North Capitol Street, turn left on Evarts Street and continue walking straight to where the streets ends at the cemetery. Turn right onto the alleyway.

featured are I Wish I Hadn't Worked So Hard, and I Wish I'd Had the Courage to Live a Life True to Myself.

While compact in size, the micro showcase and collection of signs prove to be substantial in meaning. The clever showcase project reminds visitors on their website that living small can be cool, stating that "it's an iPhone world, time for us to stop living in a Blackberry."

THE PENTAGON AND THE ILLUMINATI

What's in a shape?

The Pentagon, home to the Department of Defense, is an extraordinary architectural gem. When the building was completed in 1943, it was the largest office building in the world; today it remains one of the biggest, and one of the most important. While the massive structure is a marvel in itself, one more fascinating tidbit can be added to its already impressive resume.

A longtime theory surrounding the Pentagon holds that it is not just the national headquarters of the US military, but it may also be a headquarters for the Illuminati. That's right, the secretive underground society often accused of conspiring to control the world by manipulating events and placing agents in government and corporations, in hopes of amassing political power and organizing a New World Order.

THE PENTAGON AND THE ILLUMINATI

WHAT: The Pentagon, with its five-sided shape, is believed by some to be the secret headquarters for the Illuminati.

WHERE: 1400 Defense Pentagon Washington, DC

COST: Free

PRO TIP: There is no public parking so visitors should plan on using Metrorail, as the Pentagon has its own dedicated metro stop.

The architectural design of the five-sided Pentagon mirrors that of a pentagram, the symbol frequently associated with Freemasonry, the teachings of the fraternal order of Free and Accepted Masons, believed by some to be a far-reaching worldwide secret society. Conspiracy theorists believe that the Pentagon's repetitive design, consisting of concentric pentagrams, symbolizes the occult.

Others, however, maintain that its unique design was selected to maximize space. In fact, it's been shown that the shape of a

An ariel view of the sprawling Pentagon, an architectural masterpiece. Photo courtesy of Lance Cpl. Quinn Hurt.

pentagon results in shorter walking distances within the building than in a rectangle. Further dispelling illuminati theories, the first building location for the Pentagon was Arlington Farms, a pentagon-shaped structure. When the site location fell through, design plans were already underway, nixing any ideas of changing the shape.

Whether you choose to believe the (much) more exciting theory of an illuminati connection or its carefully planned, efficient design, one thing's certain: The Pentagon is a remarkable structure that is as prominent as it is intriguing.

Pentagon tours are offered Monday through Friday and must be reserved at least 14 days in advance and no more than 90 days in advance. The 60-minute tour covers about 1.5 miles inside the building, so wear your walking shoes!

FOAMHENGE: NOT YOUR ENVIRONMENTALIST'S MONUMENT

Where can you find a replica of Stonehenge made entirely out of Styrofoam?

Across the pond in Salisbury, England, stands arguably the world's most prehistoric monument, Stonehenge. The mysterious stone circle monument has bewildered archaeologists and historians for centuries. Perhaps not as mystifying, but engrossing nonetheless, stands its identical twin approximately 3,600 miles away—but instead of being comprised of stone, it's constructed entirely of Styrofoam. Foamhenge, a full-size replica of the ancient archaeological site, may not be a favorite among environmentalists, historians, or traditionalists, but few can argue that it's not a fascinating site to be seen. Those intrigued by this curious roadside attraction need only drive about 30 minutes outside of DC to the suburban town of Centreville, Virginia.

The mammoth monument was created by fiberglass artist Mark Cline of Enchanted Castle Studio in 2004. It was located in Northern Bridge, Virginia, until 2016 when it was moved to its new and current home at Centreville's Cox Farms. Cline's ingenious creation is an exact copy of the original Stonehenge. The artist used enormous Styrofoam blocks that look like real stone, even to those standing a short distance away. Each Styrofoam block is

---

In 2012, Mark Cline was commissioned by Alabama billionaire George Barber to build a second Stonehenge replica, called Bamahenge, which is currently on display in Elberta, Alabama.

Walking by Foamhenge, an exact replica of the world-famous Stonehenge. Photos courtesy of Mark Cline.

FOAMHENGE

WHAT: An exact replica of the world-famous Stonehenge made entirely out of Styrofoam

WHERE: Cox Farms: 15621 Braddock Rd., Centreville, VA

COST: Included with admission for Fall Festival and Fields of Fear visitors. Ticket prices vary.

PRO TIP: Foamhenge is closed from late December to late April. Throughout the rest of the year it's open on most Saturdays. Visit their website for more information: coxfarms.com/about/foamhenge

secured into the ground and sealed with cement. Cline went to great lengths to ensure that each Styrofoam "stone" matched the shape of its counterpart in England by fact-checking his plans and measurements with a Stonehenge tour guide. He even went as far as consulting a local "psychic detective" to help him position Foamhenge so that it is astronomically accurate.

While traveling to Stonehenge may not be possible for everyone living in the DC region, a relatively short jaunt to its Styrofoam identical twin may be the next best thing.

LIVING IN A DC BARBIE WORLD

Where in the nation's capital can you find a collection of Barbies celebrating seasonal holidays and advocating political activism?

DC area residents and tourists who have had their fill of visiting countless museums, monuments, and memorials will be thrilled to know that not every DC site revolves around history and government, and not every point of interest leads with the title *National* or *US*. Welcome to DC's Barbie Pond on Avenue Q, a quirky, odd, and sometimes even provocative attraction prominently displayed along a charming tree-lined street in the Logan Circle neighborhood.

The Barbie pond is a collection of Barbie dolls positioned around a pond in the anonymous artist's front yard. The whacky and revered installation rotates monthly, often reflecting pop culture trends, seasons and holidays, and of course DC's pervasive political scene. The unconventional artist clearly devotes a great amount of thought, time, and energy to create topical, progressive, and engaging displays.

While all themed presentations are creative and zany, some are more elaborate and eccentric than others. Themes run the gamut, ranging from holiday-themed dioramas depicting Valentine's Day, Cinco de Mayo, and Halloween to more politically charged themes like welcoming the Obamas when they moved into the

Political and fun-time themes showcased at Dupont Circle's quirky and revered Barbie Pond. Photos courtesy of Barbie Pond.

neighborhood post-presidency and Barbies holding "VOTE" signs while a Barbie candidate delivers a campaign speech at a podium. Other popular displays celebrating Gay Pride and activism are regularly showcased.

The offbeat attraction has been a treasured neighborhood fixture since 2014, drawing visitors and admirers from across the country. Its fanbase doesn't end there; its Instagram account has over 18,000 followers and counting. Moreover, The Barbie Pond on Avenue Q has become so popular that it's now featured on TripAdvisor and Google Maps.

The Barbie Pond is so beloved by its neighbors that when one neighbor moved, he left a gift of a Ken and Barbie set with a note reading, "After 8+ years in this neighborhood I'm moving out of DC. I wanted to leave you with a little something to say thank you for all of the joy you have brought me."

KEEP IT IN THE VAULT

Why was First Lady Dolley Madison interred in the Congressional Cemetery's Public Vault for two years?

Congressional Cemetery is a National Historic Landmark that contains the remains of many prominent government officials and military veterans. In its center stands the Public Vault, a temporary holding crypt for the remains of individuals while funeral arrangements are made. Over 3,000 individuals have been interred here, including three presidents, one vice president, and two first ladies. Many stay here for only one to two days, since it was never intended to be used for long-term stays. So, why was Dolley Madison interred in the Public Vault for two years, making her the longest known interment of the vault?

Dolley Madison was a trailblazer. She helped define the role of First Lady, was often credited with helping advance James Madison's career, and perhaps most notably, saved a historic portrait of George Washington from being burned by British troops during the War of 1812. While the Madisons were among the elite, they weren't immune to falling on hard times. As James Madison's health began to deteriorate, he prepared his presidential papers to help secure financial security for Dolley after his death. Their son Payne's recklessness, however, destroyed their finances. Payne's alcoholism, frivolous inheritance spending, and struggles with employment forced Dolley to sell the family's properties to pay his debts. After selling part of her late husband's papers, she was finally able to rise out of the family's deep financial woes and set the remaining money

---

President William Henry Harrison spent nearly twice as long in the Public Vault than he served as president. He died a mere 32 days into his term and was interred in the vault for almost three months.

The Public Vault at Congressional Cemetery, the temporary holding crypt for the remains of individuals awaiting burial. Photo courtesy of Tim Evanson.

PUBLIC VAULT AT CONGRESSIONAL CEMETERY

WHAT: Congressional Cemetery's temporary holding crypt where First Lady Dolley Madison was interred for two years

WHERE: 1801 E St. SE, Washington, DC

COST: Free

PRO TIP: Grounds are open every day from dusk to dawn.

aside in a trust and out of Payne's reach. Ultimately, her efforts weren't enough to shield her against further financial despair.

When Dolley Madison died in 1849, she was interred in the Public Vault for two years because her family ran out of money. After enough funds were finally raised, James Causten, Dolley Madison's niece's father-in-law, had her body transferred to the Causten family vault across the path. She remained there until her final interment at the family cemetery at the Montepelier estate in 1858, where she was laid to rest next to her husband.

SEEING DOUBLE: A HIDDEN MINI REPLICA

Where can you find a small-scale replica of the Washington Monument?

Perhaps no other monument in DC encapsulates the nation's capital's history and patriotism more than the Washington Monument. As a national symbol honoring the country's first president, the Monument has been a long-standing favorite landmark among both DC residents and tourists. Each year approximately 800,000 visitors flock to the 550-foot-tall obelisk stone structure. Fans of the Monument will be thrilled to learn that there is not only one Washington Monument to marvel at, but actually two! Visitors can double their fun by uncovering a hidden 12-foot replica of the monument, buried underneath a nearby manhole cover.

Officially known as Bench Mark A, the underground duplicate actually serves as a Geodetic Control Point that's primarily used by surveyors. It's part of the system of a million control points across the nation that assists the National Geodetic Survey (NGS) synchronize all of the government's maps. When it was selected as a Geodetic Control Point, the underground monument copy was somewhat of an unusual choice. Typically, items like metal cups or rods that are planted into the ground are used, not mini monuments.

MINI WASHINGTON MONUMENT REPLICA

WHAT: A 12-foot hidden replica of the famed Washington Monument

WHERE: Buried under a manhole cover just south of the Washington Monument, which is located at 2 15th St. NW, Washington, DC

COST: Free

PRO TIP: Those interested in seeing it should find the nearest park ranger (the National Mall is teeming with them!) to uncover it.

The mini Washington Monument replica is buried under a manhole cover near the National Mall. Photos courtesy of the NOAA's National Geodetic Survery.

The mini monument was deposited in the 1880s as part of a ground leveling program. The level of the ground was significantly lower at that time, with considerable portions of the Washington Monument foundation still visible above ground. The smaller-scaled replica used to be above ground before being enclosed in a brick chimney and buried. It's still used for surveying reasons; however, many have either forgotten about it or aren't aware of its existence.

In February 2019, the National Park Service unveiled the mini monument to the public for the first time. Visitors were able to see the Washington Monument replica that had been hiding underground. The replica's visibility was short-lived; shortly after its reveal, it was concealed again underneath its manhole cover.

YOU CAN LEAD A MAN TO WATER

What's one sure-fire way to drink your recommended 8 glasses of water each day?

Water is life, at least according to Henry D. Cogswell. In the late 1800s, Cogswell, a dentist from San Francisco, spent much of his life as a crusader in the temperance movement, an organized social movement that fought against the consumption of alcohol. As a leading force behind the movement, Cogswell set out to design and commission a series of temperance fountains in the belief that if individuals had access to clean drinking water, they would be more likely to abstain from consuming alcohol.

In 1882, Cogswell donated a temperance fountain to the District. It was strategically placed at a central location: Seventh and Pennsylvania Avenue, across the street from a market and close to "Hooker's Division," today known as Federal Triangle. The fountain was intended to encourage people to drink water, not whiskey, a counterpoint to the abundance of bars along the avenue enticing passersby as well as those in the neighborhood to engage with streetwalkers.

The fountain is comprised of four stone columns that support a canopy on whose sides the words *Faith, Hope, Charity,* and

---

Henry Cogswell's fountains were not always well-received, as many believed they were repulsive self-serving monuments to the inventor himself. Some fountains, including one installed in San Francisco, featured life-sized statues of Cogswell holding a glass of water in one hand and the Temperance Pledge in the other. San Francisco's fountain was torn down by a hostile crowd in 1900.

The Temperance Fountain prominently stands in the middle of Indiana Plaza. Photo courtesy of the National Park Service.

TEMPERANCE FOUNTAIN

WHAT: One of the few remaining fountains that was designed to promote drinking water instead of alcohol during the 19th- and early 20th-century Temperance Movement.

WHERE: 678 Indiana Ave. NW, Washington, DC, in the heart of Indiana Plaza

COST: Free

PRO TIP: Wealthy Henry Cogswell ultimately paid for the installment of sixteen temperance fountains around the country.

Temperance are engraved. A life-sized statue of a heron is perched atop the canopy, and the central piece is a pair of intertwined dolphins. Initially, visitors were supposed to drink ice water that poured directly from the dolphins' snouts. Cogswell installed a brass cup that hung from a chain under the dolphins. The city quickly tired of having to replenish the ice and disconnected the supply pipes.

Over a century later, many cities across the United States have removed these fountains, as they were deemed unhygienic and obsolete. The fountain in Washington, DC, is one of the few still standing!

FINALLY, ON THE MARK

Where and why was President James Garfield shot after only serving four months in office?

The next time you find yourself satisfying your love of art and getting your fix of Picasso and Monet paintings, take some time to locate the two markers that denote the site of President James Garfield's unusual assassination. The markers are situated near the south entrance of the National Gallery of Art's West Building, which is where the Baltimore and Potomac Railroad Station previously stood.

On July 2, 1881, the United States' 20th president, who had only served as president for four months, was shot by lawyer Charles J. Guiteau, a resentful and unstable man seeking to gain political power, notoriety, and revenge. Guiteau had stalked Garfield for several months prior to that night. After delivering a few small local speeches supporting Garfield during the election, Guiteau believed that he was responsible for Garfield's victory. He began sending Garfield letters and eventually moved from Chicago to Washington. He made demands of the president, including for a post in Paris even though he had no prior experience and did not speak French. Angered and fueled by Garfield's dismissal and rejection, Guiteau set out to shoot Garfield at the present-day site of the National Gallery of Art. He later explained that he was lying in bed one evening when God told him to kill the president so that Vice President Chester A. Arthur

---

SITE OF PRESIDENT GARFIELD'S BIZARRE ASSASSINATION

WHAT: Two recently placed markers at the present-day National Gallery of Art marking the odd assassination of President James Garfield

WHERE: National Gallery of Art; Constitution Avenue NW, Washington, DC

COST: Free

PRO TIP: The markers are positioned on the National Mall nearest to the south entrance of the National Gallery of Art's West Building.

Outside of the National Gallery of Art, where two markers indicate the spot where President James Garfield was assassinated. Photo courtesy of Washington.org.

could bring Republican principals back to the United States and save the country. Guiteau was found guilty of murder and sentenced to execution.

While the two markers mark the assassination site today, they were only placed there recently. A campaign by historians and year-long deliberations procured these two signs, finally bringing recognition to the site. Prior to their placement, Garfield was the only assassinated US president without a marker at the location he was shot.

Garfield did not die until September 19, more than two months after being shot. Not understanding the severe effects of germ-spreading and infections, doctors spent months after his shooting probing for the bullet, inserting unsterilized instruments and fingers in his back. Garfield was also unable to eat any of the rich meals that were still being prepared for him, causing him to grow gaunt and eventually die.

43

ASK AND SAY YES

Where in Washington, DC, can you follow in JFK's and Jackie's engagement footsteps?

As a cherished Georgetown institution dating back to 1933, Martin's Tavern is the community's oldest family-run restaurant. Its old-DC charm, neighborhood-friendly appeal, and warm and inviting ambience have drawn patrons for close to a century. Add that it also served as the location of John F. Kennedy Jr's proposal to Jacqueline Bouvier, and it's easy to see why Martin's has been a perennial favorite among both locals and tourists.

On June 24, 1953, the young senator from Massachusetts proposed to his beautiful girlfriend at the historic and intimate Georgetown tavern. Over the years, however, doubt began to arise about whether Martin's was actually the site of the engagement. Alternate stories surfaced, including that Kennedy had proposed over the phone or by telegram, or at a restaurant in Boston. After years of skepticism and speculation, the story was finally corroborated in 2015, when then-98-year-old Marion Smoak confirmed that he was enjoying a martini at the bar on the same night that Kennedy proposed. Although the engagement took place in a public setting, the event was a quiet one, absent of any grand gestures or words, or bended knee.

Booth number 3, where Kennedy popped the question, has since been dubbed the "the engagement booth" and is proudly adorned with a brass plaque. It only seemed fitting that two years after Smoak's announcement Martin's would present Smoak with his very own plaque to commemorate the historic moment.

Many argue that JFK's proposal was as politically charged as it was romantic, so it's unclear if the proposal was a traditional one.

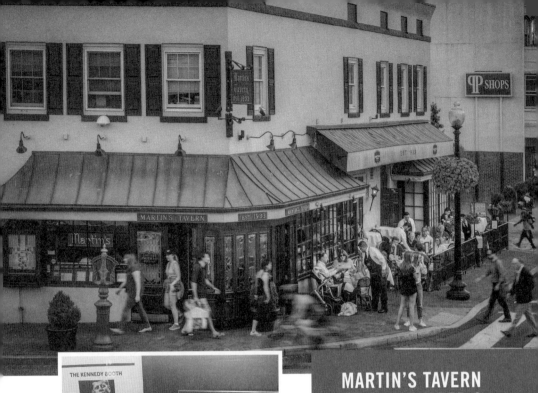

Top: *The historic Georgetown gem, Martin's Tavern. Photo courtesy of Sam Kittner.* Inset: *A commemorative plaque hangs inside the booth marking where President John F. Kennedy proposed to Jacqueline Bouvier. Photo courtesy of Martin's Tavern.*

MARTIN'S TAVERN BOOTH NUMBER 3

WHAT: The site of John F. Kennedy Jr's proposal to then-girlfriend Jacqueline Bouvier

WHERE: 1264 Wisconsin Ave. NW, Washington, DC

COST: Dependent on how hungry and thirsty you are

PRO TIP: The staff keeps chilled bottles of champagne in stock to toast any lovebird couples looking to follow in the Kennedy's footsteps.

Engraved on Smoak's plaque are the words "The night didn't know his future and what it would bring. In hindsight, it was great fun to witness a part of history."

SORRY FOR STEALING, BUT PLEASE TIGHTEN YOUR SECURITY

What valuable and costly lesson did the Phillips Collection learn?

Mention the words "art heist" and there's a good chance that a slew of action-packed movies like *The Thomas Crown Affair* and *Entrapment* conjure up to mind. Well, it turns out that art museum thefts aren't exclusive to Hollywood films; sometimes they occur right in your neighborhood, sometimes the stolen masterpieces turn up in unexpected places, and sometimes the thefts are executed to teach the museum a lesson.

Located in DC's prestigious Dupont Circle neighborhood, The Phillips Collection is home to more than 5,000 pieces in styles ranging from French impressionism and American modernism to contemporary art. The collection includes works by an array of renowned artists such as Georgia O'Keefe, Edgar Degas, and Pablo Picasso. It is regarded as the nation's oldest modern art museum.

In January 1983, the typically quiet museum was anything but; instead it became the center of an art heist, bustling with commotion and confusion. A museum guard became suspicious when he noticed a man leaving the museum with his arms wrapped around a bunched-up

ART HEIST AT THE PHILLIPS COLLECTION

WHAT: A small art museum where a statue valued at $35,000 was stolen to bring attention to the museum's lax security

WHERE: 1600 21st St. NW, Washington, DC

COST: Free Tuesdays–Fridays when no ticketed exhibition is on view

Adults: $10; Students and visitors 62 and over: $8

PRO TIP: The nearest metro station is DuPont Circle along the red line.

The Phillips Collection, a small but beloved art museum located in DC's prestigious Dupont Circle. Left photo courtesy of Lee Stalsworth for the Phillips Collection. Right photo courtesy of Robert Lautman for the Phillips Collection.

tweed coat. It didn't take long for the museum to realize that the man, accompanied by a female companion, had stolen "Virgin Alsace," a 1920 statue by Antoine Bourdelle valued at $35,000. The next day, the museum received a phone call from an anonymous woman stating that the statue could be found in an alley behind a gas station at 18th and S streets NW. Members of the museum staff, including director Laughlin Phillips, hurried to the site and found the marble statue stuffed inside of a trash bag. Included in the bag was a note, written in block letters on yellow legal paper, criticizing the museum for their negligent security while simultaneously apologizing for the inconvenience. Talk about learning a valuable (and costly) lesson!

In 1975, a collection of 21 prints worth more than $70,000 were stolen from the museum by its curator, Richard Friedman. Friedman resigned from the gallery after investigators had discovered the theft. He later returned some of the prints.

A WHOLE LOTTA JUNK: THE VANADU ART HOUSE

Who is the mastermind behind the Vanadu Art House, a marriage of art, junk, and ingenuity?

Approximately seven miles outside of Washington, DC, stands a treasure trove of junk—junk that is simultaneously art, that is. In 2007, museum conservator Clarke Bedford transformed his average-sized home into an elaborately designed art house brimming with intricately adorned objects and recycled metal oddities.

Bedford dubbed his unique art home Vanadu to pay tribute to Samuel Taylor Coleridge's poem "Kubla Khan," which surfaced from an opium-charged dream about the ancient Chinese city of Xanadu, once ruled by Mongol emperor Kublai Khan. Bedford's remarkable art house is a cornucopia of antiques, mosaics, sculptures, mirrors, and well, you guessed it, junk. An array of hand-made assemblages including old pictures made of cut-up license plates and a woman's face covered with glass grace the grounds. Some of the home's more eccentric items include a statue of philosopher John Locke, a horned wooden owl, and a German language globe stuffed inside a rusted horn.

Bedford has also used his ingenuity to build four fully operating art cars from an amalgamation of materials, including various car parts, washing machine pieces, and moose antlers. The most famous of the cars is the Vanadu Ford, embellished with accents like horns, vases, and graveyard spires. While Bedford's art house is commonly

Clarke Bedford's avant-garde art junk house and cars adorned with metal scraps, mirrors, moose antlers, and other oddities. Top photo courtesy of Clarke Bedford. Inset photo courtesy of Sandra Cole.

referred to as "Vanadu," he also calls the conglomeration of recycled materials the Assemblage Cottage, pronounced in the French manner, "As-sem-blage Co-ttage," so that it rhymes.

Clarke Bedford enjoys riding in his intricately embellished cars, even if it is "like driving down the road in a garbage can."

THE PLANE! THE PLANE!

Where in the DC area can you fulfill your aviation dreams?

Aviation enthusiasts, those stimulated by roaring and ear-piercing sounds, and those simply dreaming of escaping to faraway destinations should look no further than Gravelly Point Park, a small grassy park located a mere 100 feet north of Ronald Reagan Washington National Airport. It's here in this delightful park in which both aircraft lovers and travel addicts can convene to witness commercial planes soaring overhead throughout the course of the day.

Situated along the George Washington Parkway in northern Virginia, the attractive picnic spot is where arriving planes descend to their landing strips. Flights arriving at the capital city travel over the Potomac River to reduce noise disturbances to the city. The park's proximity to the north end of Reagan's runway 1/19 makes it one of the premier spots in the United States for airplane sightings. Spectators willing to brave the thunderous noise are rewarded with unobstructed views of aircraft departing and arriving into the airport.

While flight tracking is the primary draw here, Gravelly Point Park attracts more than just aviation fanatics. It's also a wonderful place to enjoy a picnic lunch, throw a frisbee or football, walk your dog, or ride a bike while surrounded by

GRAVELLY POINT PARK

WHAT: A park near Ronald Reagan Washington National Airport that's one of the best places in the US for aircraft viewing

WHERE: George Washington Parkway, Arlington, VA

COST: Entrance and parking are free to the public.

PRO TIP: Gravelly Point is only accessible heading north on the GW Parkway.

Ronald Reagan Washington National Airport and a sweeping view of the George Washington Parkway in Arlington, Virginia. Top photo courtesy of Washington.org. Inset photo courtesy of the National Park Service.

arresting scenic views. Regardless of your reason to visit, you're guaranteed to be flying high in this picturesque park.

The area known as Gravelly Point was where Captain John Alexander built a home called Abingdon in 1746. Abington was purchased by John Parke Custis, the adopted stepson of President George Washington. It was the birthplace of Washington's granddaughter, Eleanor Parke Custis.

A GRAVE SITUATION: HOW ROBERT E. LEE'S GARDEN BECAME A GRAVEYARD

Why was General Robert E. Lee's Arlington garden converted into a cemetery during the Civil War?

Arlington Cemetery is one of the nation's most famous and historic cemeteries, welcoming over three million visitors each year. Over 400,000 individuals have been laid to rest here, including active duty military and retired reservists, recipients of the military's highest honors, former POWs, and two US presidents. The expansive cemetery, which covers an astounding 624 acres, has held the remains of those killed in combat since the Civil War. It may come as a surprise to learn that Confederate leader Robert E. Lee's former home was once at the center of this world-renowned cemetery.

After Lee resigned from the US Army to command the Confederate forces, the US Army began to occupy his land. In 1864, the government purchased the property. As a result of an overwhelming number of Civil War causalities, the property was soon converted to a national cemetery. Fearful that Lee would return after the war to recoup his land and remove the graves, some Union leaders hoped to deter Lee by burying multiple casualties close to his home. By August of 1864, the graves of 26 fallen soldiers encircled Lee's rose garden.

Robert E. Lee is buried at Lee Chapel in Lexington, Virginia, not in Arlington Cemetery where his former home once stood.

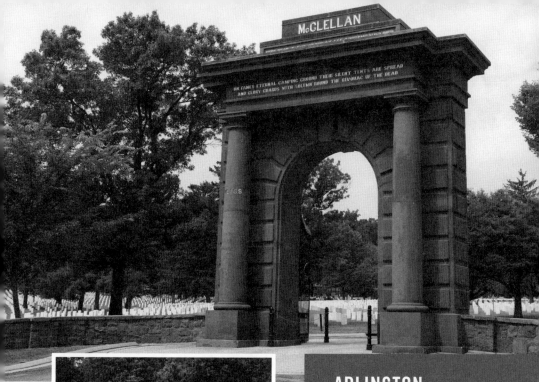

Top: *McClellan Gate marks the entrance of the renowned Arlington Cemetery.* Inset: *Tombstones of the brave men and women who have fought and died for our country. Photos courtesy of Arlington National Cemetery.*

ARLINGTON CEMETERY

WHAT: The United States' most important burial ground, which was the former home of Confederate general Robert E. Lee before it was converted into a graveyard

WHERE: Arlington National Cemetery, Arlington, VA

COST: Free

PRO TIP: Visitors can see the graves every day of the year, from 8 a.m. to 7 p.m. in the summer and until 5 p.m. through the remainder of the year.

While this act may seem a bit outlandish and aggressive, at one point Lee and his brother were indeed planning on returning to the estate, as well as dismantling the graves. Ultimately, Lee never did return to his Arlington home, and instead moved to Lexington, Virginia before dying five years later.

ONE TOUGH TREE

Where can you find a tree that survived an atomic bomb?

It may not receive the same kind of notoriety as heavy-hitter museums like the Air and Space Museum and Natural History Museum, but that doesn't mean the Bonsai Museum isn't just as amazing and unique. Although miniature in size, the National Arboretum's impressive collection of bonsai trees packs a whole lot of punch, and one in particular represents history that spans across centuries.

The first of its kind in the world, The National Bonsai and Penjing Museum has been home to over 100 specimens since its inception in the 1970s. The open-air museum includes trees from Japan, China, and North America. Similar to the generous gift of cherry trees that Japan bestowed upon Washington, DC, in March 1912, Japan's Nippon Bonsai Association gifted 53 bonsai trees to the US National Arboretum in July 1976.

Many of these beautiful green miniature plants are steeped in history. The imperial pine has been flourishing since 1795. It's one of two identical bonsai that once adorned the Imperial Household in Japan. Emperor Hirohito gifted one tree to the United States and kept the other in Japan.

Proving to be one of the oldest and resilient of the bonsai is the nearly 400-year-old Yamaki Pine, which managed to survive the dropping of the Atomic Bomb in Hiroshima. On that fateful morning

NATIONAL BONSAI AND PENJING MUSEUM

WHAT: A collection of bonsai and penjing trees, including one that survived the bombing of Hiroshima

WHERE: The National Arboretum: 3501 New York Ave. NE, Washington, DC

COST: Free

PRO TIP: Various events are offered at the Bonsai and Penjing Museum, including working with bonsai masters, taking yoga classes amid the trees, and drawing classes.

The famed and resilient bonsai tree continues to bask in the sunshine, even after nearly 400 years. Photo courtesy of the US National Arboretum.

of Thursday, August 6, 1945, bonsai expert Masaru Yamaki's home was one of many that was impacted by the devastating explosion. Yamaki and his family, as well as his cherished bonsai trees, miraculously survived the blast. This astounding feat was unknown for 25 years until two of Masaru Yamaki's grandsons made a surprise visit to the Arboretum in search of the tree they had heard about their entire lives.

Two years after Masaru Yamaki's grandsons visited the Arboretum, Yamaki's daughter also made the trip to view her father's revered tree.

WHAT LIES BENEATH

Where in Washington, DC, can you find subterranean crypts, chapels, and relics?

While many people across the globe may be familiar with the world-renowned catacombs of Paris and Rome, they may be surprised that similar subterranean passageways also exist in Washington, DC. Hidden underneath the resplendent Franciscan Monastery of the Holy Land in America are fascinating catacombs just waiting to be explored.

Consecrated in September 1924, the monastery's 15 chapels and tranquil gardens have been drawing visitors for decades. The underground catacombs, however, are not nearly as known or visited as their European counterparts. The catacombs were built in the late 1800s by a group of monks who wanted to offer a spiritual experience to Americans who could not afford the trip abroad. The mysterious catacombs are replicas of the tombs and graves in Rome.

Narrow and dimly lit passageways lead to Roman crypts, statues, and chapels. One chapel of note is the Purgatory Chapel, designed to serve as a reminder of the inevitability of death, and in contrast, eternal life. Perhaps the catacombs' most intriguing relics are the remains of two deceased saints: Saint Benignus, a Roman soldier beheaded in the second century for his faith, and Saint Innocent, a six- or seven-year-old boy who became a martyr when he was killed for being a Christian. Saint Benignus' head

---

To accurately recreate the catacombs and its replicas, the Monastery's architect, Aristide Leonori, visited Italy and other religious locations where he took painstaking measurements and copious notes.

The beautiful grounds of the Franciscan Monastery of the Holy Land in America. Photo courtesy of Loslazos via Creative Commons.

remains in Rome, while his bones are in the DC catacombs. Saint Innocent's remains are sealed within a glass case illuminated by electric light.

Visitors wishing to explore these eerie and hidden catacombs can thank the well-meaning monks for saving them the long flight and expensive airfare.

CATACOMBS AT THE FRANCISCAN MONASTERY OF THE HOLY LAND IN AMERICA

WHAT: Underground passageways that are replicas of Roman graves and tombs

WHERE: The Franciscan Monastery of the Holy Land in America: 1400 Quincy St. NE, Washington, DC

COST: Free

PRO TIP: Ask a staff member for a free guided tour from 10 a.m. to 3 p.m. daily.

EAT, SLEEP, SPY: ESPIONAGE AT THE MAYFLOWER HOTEL

How did DC's landmark hotel become a prominent meeting spot for spies around the world?

Regarded as one the most historic and iconic hotels in the nation's capital, The Mayflower Hotel has hosted a long line of distinguished guests, including presidents, royalty, dignitaries, and celebrities.

ESPIONAGE AT THE MAYFLOWER HOTEL

WHAT: A DC landmark and historic hotel that has served as the setting for multiple planned spy operations.

WHERE: The Mayflower Hotel: 1127 Connecticut Ave. NW, Washington, DC

COST: Room rates and dining/bar options at the hotel's Edgar Bar & Kitchen vary.

PRO TIP: The hotel is easily accessible from two metro stations: Farragut West and Farragut North.

Some of its most beguiling guests, however, have been the many spies who have worked, dined, and slept here. The stately hotel has been an espionage haven for decades, dating back to World War II and continuing into recent years.

In 1942, German spy George John Dasch checked into room 351 with hopes of meeting with FBI Director J. Edgar Hoover to divulge his spy mission, Operation Pastorius. When Dasch called the FBI to expose the Nazi mission, the FBI treated it as a scam and dismissed him. While Hoover did not end up meeting with Dasch, an FBI agent did, resulting in Dasch leading the FBI to the other seven saboteurs, who were working in New York City. Dasch was ultimately pardoned by President Truman, while six of the convicted saboteurs were executed in DC's electric chair.

Nearly two decades later during the 1960s, CIA officers used the hotel's lobby as a meeting point to perfect a new tradecraft method, known as the "brush pass," which entailed two agents

The Mayflower Hotel: DC's iconic, historic, and grand hotel. Photos courtesy of The Mayflower Hotel, Autograph Collection.

"meeting" and quickly exchanging information, documents, or equipment. Most recently in 2009, NASA scientist Stewart Nozette was arrested at the Mayflower for attempting to sell classified satellite information to agents he thought were Israeli spies.

The Mayflower's close proximity to the White House and legendary reputation for being a convivial hotspot make for an ideal location for spies and espionage fanatics to gather and test just how safe some secrets truly are.

The Mayflower Hotel has also been the location of other Washington, DC, scandals, including the site where the famous photograph of President Bill Clinton hugging then-intern Monica Lewinsky was taken.

WHERE FALLEN SHIPS ARE LAID TO REST

Where in the Potomac River can you explore over 200 shipwrecks?

Kayakers and canoers exploring the open waters of the Potomac River may find themselves confronted with a ghostly sight far beyond its rampant pollution issues. Near the shores of Mallows Bay, a small bay on the Maryland side of the river, lies what's known to be the largest shipwreck armada in the Western Hemisphere. Over the last century, the bay's turbid waters have become home to nearly 230 fallen ships, creating an enormous fleet graveyard.

When the United States entered World War I in 1917, 1,000 wooden steamships were commissioned for construction to help boost the number of transport vessels needed. Steel was not in abundance at the time, so its use was limited to the ships that would actually see battle. Due to time constraints, the wooden ships were hastily and shoddily built, falling far below the standard of being ready to be used in wartime. In fact, not one of these poorly crafted vessels ever even crossed the ocean. The following year Germany surrendered, and the availability of steel increased, causing the ill-conceived wooden ships to become abandoned and obsolete. The decaying remnants of the nearly forgotten ships continue to occupy the muddy waters of Mallows Bay to this day. While a few attempts have been made to remove pieces of the wreckage, they have been mostly unsuccessful due to high costs and the enormity of the task.

Several of the abandoned ships are visible from the shore. Kayakers and canoeists who paddle up and through the wreckage will ultimately get the best views.

Mallows Bay, a small bay on the Maryland side of the Potomac River that's home to over 200 shipwrecks. Photo courtesy of Maryland GovPics via Creative Commons.

THE ABANDONED SHIPWRECKS OF MALLOWS BAY

WHAT: Over 200 ships decaying in the Potomac River that were originally built to be used in World War I

WHERE: Wilson Landing Road, Nanjemoy, MD

COST: Free

PRO TIP: Exercise caution when paddling among the wreckage. Sharp metal pieces sometimes poke through the waves.

In the 1960s, researchers began to evaluate the environmental effects of the shipwrecks on the river and its inhabitants. It was determined that the wooden shipwrecks were non-toxic and had in fact become a foundation for a flourishing ecosystem. The ghostly ships have managed to bring new life to the river, completing the circle of life!

HANNIBAL LECTER HAS MET HIS MATCH

Why is there a brass plaque honoring a self-confessed cannibal at the National Press Club?

Founded in 1908, the esteemed National Press Club serves as a professional organization and social gathering place for journalists and communications professionals. Over the past century, the National Press Club has transformed from a refuge for reporters looking to relax and enjoy a drink into a leading world organization for journalists and a venue for both professional and social events. An extensive collection of plaques and photographs adorn many of the club's walls, honoring a wide array of notable individuals from throughout the club's history. Perhaps its oddest and most questionable plaque hangs in the penthouse restaurant and bar, Reliable Source, honoring Alferd Packer, a convicted gold-prospecting cannibal.

ALFERD PACKER PLAQUE AT THE NATIONAL PRESS CLUB

WHAT: A hanging brass plaque dedicated to infamous cannibal Alferd Packer

WHERE: 529 14th St. NW, Washington, DC

COST: Free

PRO TIP: Club Hours are Monday–Friday from 7 a.m. to 11 p.m. and Saturday from 10 a.m. to 9 p.m.

The National Press Club was not the original home of Packer's bizarre plaque. It was initially hung at the Department of Agriculture in 1977 under the orders of Agriculture Secretary Robert Bergland. While battling the General Services Administration over replacing an unpopular food service contractor inside his headquarters, Bergland decided to retaliate by dedicating the cafeteria to a cannibal. He invited the media to expose and embarrass the organization and even went as far as telling Barbara Walters on ABC News that

The National Press Club's restaurant, where a plaque hangs remembering cannibal Alferd Packer. Photos courtesy of Alan Kotok for the National Press Club.

THE ALFERD PACKER

MEMORIAL GRILL

IN MEMORY OF STAN WESTON 1984

Alferd Packer "exemplifies the spirit and the fare of this Agricultural Department cafeteria." Bergland's vengeful performance was blasted across news circuits and printed in newspapers across the country. Bergland ultimately won when the GSA contract was canceled, and as a result, he took the plaque down.

Later, a bewildered journalist was given the plaque by Stan Weston, the USDA's public affairs officer responsible for creating a contest to name the USDA's new cafeteria. The brass plaque, which was eventually altered to commemorate Westin, now hangs at the National Press Club. At their restaurant, diners can find an Alferd Packer certified angus beef burger on their menu.

During the Gold Rush, Alferd Packer joined a group of men looking for fortune in Colorado. Alone in the wilderness and trapped in heavy snows, Packer and his team struggled to find food and were eventually forced to resort to cannibalism.

DIGGING, BIGAMY, AND COMPULSION IN THE UNDERGROUND

What is the story behind the discovery of 200 feet of tunnels in Dupont Circle?

Many DC residents are familiar with the Dupont Underground, a hip and unique space that has recently become home to an avant-garde public arts scene. Less known in the same neighborhood is yet another underground system of tunnels; its history, however, is much more perplexing and downright bizarre.

In 1924, a subterranean labyrinthine tunnel system was discovered in Dupont Circle after the weight of a truck caused it to fall into the tunnels. Harrison Dyar, a prominent Smithsonian entomologist greatly respected in his field, as well as a bigamist, was responsible for the creation of the 200 feet of meandering tunnels. Dyar dug these tunnels between two of his DC properties, one in Dupont Circle, the other south of the National Mall. The impressive electric-lit tunnels were "broad enough for a man to walk with ease." Scattered throughout the labyrinth were empty alcohol bottles and old newspaper clippings on German submarine activities.

A great amount of speculation arose regarding the reason behind these intricate tunnels. Was Dyar executing top-secret

---

Highly regarded in his field of entomology, Harrion Dyar is the name and reason behind Dyar's Law, a principle citing head size in larvae as a predictor of the number and nature of stages in insects' full life cycles. The law is still widely used today.

HARRISON DYAR'S UNDERGROUND TUNNEL SYSTEM

WHAT: A subterranean maze-like tunnel system dug by Smithsonian entomologist Harrison Dyar

WHERE: Extending from Dupont Circle to just south of the National Mall

COST: These tunnels are sealed with concrete and are no longer passable.

PRO TIP: Unfortunately, Dyar's tunnels died with his legend and have been sealed with concrete.

Exploring the fascinating and previously hidden tunnels of Harrison Dyar. Photo courtesy of the National Photo Company Collection.

experiments? Were the tunnels used for World War I spy activities? Were they another example of Dyar's many eccentricities and unconventional hobbies? Some hypothesized that the tunnels were dug to allow Dyar to travel covertly between his two families, while others believed that he dug them purely out of boredom. Dyar simply wrote the arduous digging off as a great physical workout, while many wondered if the tunnels provided Dyar with a way of relieving stress and absolving his sins of bigamy and leading a double life.

Dyar died in 1929 after suffering a stroke at his desk. Nearly a century has passed since his death, and his legend and elaborate labyrinth system continue to leave many unanswered questions.

CHEERS TO THAT!

How did the rickey become the official cocktail of our nation's capital?

Mixologists often take careful measurements in creating the perfect amalgamation of spirits, mixers, ice, and accompanying garnishes. Some bartenders, however, venture beyond the craft. Some, like Derek Brown, seek out the drink's history and significance. Such curiosity explains how Brown learned of the rickey, the cocktail that would eventually be designated Washington's official drink.

In the mid-1800s, a bartender named George A. Williamson concocted the rickey at a well-known bar called Shoomaker's, situated off of Pennsylvania Avenue NW. The cocktail was a favorite of Colonel Joseph Kyle Rickey, a Democratic lobbyist and regular Shoomaker's patron who was often credited with co-creating the drink. The colonel committed suicide in 1903, and according to his Washington Post obituary he would frequently spend time at Shoomaker's and ask Williamson for a drink comprised of whisky, one cube of ice, and seltzer. Fred Mussey, a stranger and fellow patron who would watch Rickey enjoy this drink, which was dubbed "the rickey," took the recipe to New York, ultimately resulting in the rise of the cocktail's popularity. Derek Brown, however, was dubious of the story's accuracy and began to research further, ultimately trusting author George Rothwell Brown's account. Brown suggested that a stranger told Williamson that Caribbean drinks were often made with lime halves. The stranger then proceeded to give the bartender some limes and requested that rye whiskey be substituted for rum. The next

---

Bartender Derek Brown boosted the rickey's popularity and advocated its importance as DC's native cocktail by hosting annual rickey contests and declaring July "Rickey Month."

The gin rickey: Washington, DC's famed official drink. Photo courtesy of Greg Powers for JW Marriott, Washington, DC.

THE RICKEY: WASHINGTON, DC'S OFFICIAL NATIVE COCKTAIL

WHAT: Washington's native cocktail made with either gin or bourbon, half of a lime, and carbonated water

WHERE: The rickey was designated Washington's native cocktail at the JW Marriott: 1331 Pennsylvania Ave. NW, Washington, DC

COST: $13.00

PRO TIP: The Metro Center station is the closest station to the JW Marriott.

morning, Williamson whipped up one of these cocktails, and Colonel Rickey approved.

Regardless of which account is accurate, thanks to Derek Brown, who promoted the rickey in a multitude of ways, the rickey was officially declared Washington's "native cocktail" in 2011. The event was commemorated with a ceremony dedicating a plaque in the cocktail's honor. The plaque hangs in the JW Marriott's bar. Although the Marriott is where the ceremony occurred and the location of its accompanying plaque, the hotel and its bar had no connection to the drink's creation.

BEYOND THE GRAVE: THE MYSTERY BEHIND JANE DOE'S IDENTITY

Why is there a tomb honoring an unknown female stranger in Old Town Alexandria's cemetery?

Cemeteries often evoke feelings of moroseness, loneliness, and even eeriness. Mystery, on the other hand, is not nearly as common thanks to the invention of grave markers thousands of years ago. Yet in the St. Paul's Episcopal Church section of Old Town Alexandria's cemetery, one particular grave's identity has been shrouded in mystery for over two centuries.

According to local folklore, in 1816, a young couple arrived by ship in Alexandria and rented a room at the popular Gadsby's Tavern. The wife was extremely ill, and her husband paid for a local physician to care for her under one circumstance: that his wife's identity remained unknown. The doctor honored his wishes and the couple isolated themselves at the Gadsby, rarely consorting with any townspeople or guests. The couple's seclusion led to much speculation, and rumors began to swirl. The mystery wife's condition quickly worsened, and she eventually died on October 14, 1816. Her husband borrowed money from a local merchant so that he

THE GRAVE OF AN UNIDENTIFIED FEMALE STRANGER

WHAT: An unidentified tombstone of a female stranger who died shortly after her arrival in Alexandria, Virginia, in 1816

WHERE: St. Paul's Cemetery of the St. Paul's Episcopal Church: 601 Hamilton Ave., Alexandria, VA

COST: Free

PRO TIP: From Wilkes Street, continue down Hamilton Avenue for ¼ mile and turn left at the sign for St. Paul's Cemetery. In 100 feet, make your first right. The Female Stranger grave is the third grave on the right.

Grave of the Unknown Female Stranger in St. Paul's Cemetery of the St. Paul's Episcopal Church in Alexandria, Virginia. Photo courtesy of Michael Lusk.

could bury her in town, repaying him with a check from the Bank of England that ultimately turned out to be a forgery.

Over 200 years later, the unidentified woman's tomb bears the inscription, "To the memory of a Female Stranger whose mortal sufferings terminated on the 14th day of October 1816 Aged 23 years and 8 months. This stone was placed here by her disconsolate Husband in whose arms she sighed out her latest breath and who under God did his utmost even to soothe the cold dead ear of death."

Throughout the years, a number of theories surrounding the woman's identity have emerged, including that she may have been Theodosia Burr Alston, the daughter of former Vice President Aaron Burr, who was mysteriously lost at sea in 1813.

Today the Gadsby Tavern is a museum where visitors can tour and learn about its rich history and its multiple distinguished guests, including John Adams, Thomas Jefferson, James Madison, James Monroe, Alexander Hamilton, Aaron Burr, and the Marquis de Lafayette.

GHOSTED IN DANIELS

What's the story behind a once booming town that's now a mystifying ghost town?

When visiting a ghost town, it's often difficult to imagine what stood there before. Signs of desertion and decay often cloud our ability to envision the possibility of past life and vibrancy. Daniels, once a booming industrial town in Ellicott City, Maryland, is now one of the most mystifying ghost towns in the DC area. An abandoned shell of its former self that's faded away in a deep wooded forest, the ghost town of Daniels is now sadly characterized merely by rotting wood and crumbling stone.

Straddling the Patapsco River, the town of Daniels was originally settled in 1810 when Thomas Ely and his family moved here to establish a textile mill. The area around the mill became known as Elysville. Over 40 years later, the town was bought by the family of James S. Gary and renamed Alberton in recognition of their son Albert. The mill stayed within the Gary family for nearly a century until the Daniels Company came along and purchased the entire village in 1940. $65,000 bought them 500 acres and the right to change the town's name from Alberton to Daniels. By the 1960s, Daniels had emerged as a thriving small town complete with a general store, post office, library, ball field, several churches, entertainment spots, a school, and railroad station. The textile mill was the epicenter of the town, owning much of the town's businesses and buildings. Around 90 families

In 1979, Daniels Mill was placed on the National Register of Historic Places. The Daniels Band assists in preserving the history of the abandoned town and organizes an annual reunion where participants gather to share memories.

The deserted ghost town of Daniels and its eponymous mill, which was placed on the National Register of Historic Places. Photos courtesy of Patorjk via Creative Commons.

WHAT: A forsaken ghost town that was formerly a booming industrial town

WHERE: Ellicott City, MD

COST: Free; open dawn to dusk

PRO TIP: Take Daniels Road off of Route 40 West, then navigate to Alberton Rd off of Dogwood Road. Walk along the footpath to see ruins and abandoned churches.

called Daniels home until they were forced to pack up and leave when the mill closed down in 1968. The Daniels Company had warned the townspeople several years prior that the closure of the mill was imminent and residential housing would be terminated.

As if it hadn't endured enough misfortune, four years later Daniels was further devastated when tropical storm Agnes pummeled the town. Massive flooding that utterly destroyed buildings further led to the town's demise and abandonment.

SIGNED, SEALED, BUT THANKFULLY NOT DELIVERED

How did two innocent men nearly become confined inside the cement walls of the Second Division Memorial?

There is no shortage of monuments, memorials, or other significant landmarks in Washington commemorating the many individuals who have helped shape the history and fabric of the United States.

SECOND INFANTRY DIVISION WWI MEMORIAL

WHAT: A memorial commemorating the members of the US Army who lost their lives during WWI

WHERE: President's Park, between 17th Street NW and Constitution Avenue NW, Washington, DC

COST: Free

PRO TIP: The west panel of the structure honors the fallen troops of WWII, while the east panel honors those who died in the Korean War.

Located in the President's Park, the Second Division Memorial pays tribute to those who died while serving in the second Infantry Division of the US Army during World War I. Over 60 years ago, a terrifying mistake here almost led to an irreversible and tragic disaster that would have sealed the fate of two innocent men forever.

The memorial was originally dedicated in 1936 by President Franklin D. Roosevelt to honor members of the US Army for their heroic service in World War I. The flaming swords in the memorial's center pay homage to the defense of Paris from German forces. Approximately 25 years later, two wings were added to the memorial's structure to commemorate the army's service in World War II and the Korean War.

Coinciding with the memorial's two additions in 1962, the Second Division Memorial was rededicated, and right before the dedication two homeless men unknowingly entered. The monument

Second Infantry Division WWI Memorial in President's Park. Top photo courtesy of the National Parks Service. Inset photo courtesy of David from Washington, DC, via Creative Commons.

was still under construction, and workers were about to install an eight-inch slab of granite on top of the memorial, which would cause the structure to be sealed forever. Fortunately, the workers heard newspapers crinkling inside the memorial and found the two men. Thankfully the men were able to get outside before they were tragically trapped inside the memorial forever.

The total number of Second Division casualties in World War I was about 15,000, the most of any US division.

ROUND AND ROUND: A CAROUSEL TAKES A TURN INTO THE CIVIL RIGHTS MOVEMENT

How does the National Mall's beloved carousel reflect Civil Rights history?

For decades, the National Mall's iconic carousel has been a prominent fixture on the city's most popular strip of grassy land. The lively ride draws both children and parents looking for some carefree fun and jubilant reprieve from the surrounding museums and monuments. The carousel, however, is much more than an exuberant ride; it also serves as a hopeful window into the Civil Rights Movement.

On August 28, 1963, Reverend Martin Luther King, Jr. delivered his powerful "I Have a Dream" speech before a crowd of some 250,000 people during the March on Washington. On that same day, about 45 miles away outside of Baltimore, Gwynn Oak Amusement Park discontinued segregation. An 11-month-old baby named Sharon Langley was the first African American child to go on a ride there and rode the classic carousel (which was originally located in the park) along with two white children. The three children riding the carousel together exemplified King's message of integration and racial harmony.

The carousel's owners sought out the exact horse that made history 50 years ago and decorated it with a "Freedom Riders" theme, complete with names of civil rights heroes and a brass plaque with the name of the carousel's original freedom rider, Sharon Langley.

Children and adults alike ride on the popular and historic carousel on the National Mall. Photo courtesy of Casey McAdams.

CAROUSEL ON THE NATIONAL MALL

WHAT: The historic carousel on the National Mall that represents a part of the Civil Rights history

WHERE: National Mall: Jefferson Drive SW, Washington, DC

COST: $3.50 per ride

PRO TIP: The carousel is open daily from 10 a.m. to 6 p.m.

In 1981, the famous carousel made its way to its new home on the National Mall when a Smithsonian concessionaire purchased it, unaware of its historical significance. Seven years later, Donna and Stan Hunter purchased the special carousel and have owned and operated it ever since. Fittingly, the vibrant merry-go-round stands just steps from where King delivered his history-changing speech. Today individuals from around the globe come to ride on the carousel's fancifully painted horses while listening to playful melodies, often unknowingly spinning around a piece of Civil Rights history.

THE DOG DAYS OF THE US POSTAL SYSTEM

How did an abandoned mutt become the mascot of the US Postal System, landing himself in the National Postal Museum?

In 1888, a scruffy mutt was abandoned by a postal clerk in an Albany, New York, post office. Postal workers wrapped him in postal bags to keep him warm, and so began the launch of Owney's path toward becoming the unofficial mascot of the US Postal System. The dog is so beloved by US Postal System that he landed a prominent spot in the Smithsonian National Postal Museum.

Described as a dog who was attracted to the texture and scents of mail bags, Owney soon began following mailbags everywhere. Over the next decade, he travelled by train and accompanied mail clerks around the world, travelling a staggering 140,000 miles. He soon became a good luck charm to the mail clerks who travelled with him. At a time when train accidents were common, no train that Owney had travelled on was ever in an accident. To commemorate Owney's extensive travels, he was adorned with medals and tags labelled with city names. When Owney would return to Albany, the clerks there would save the tags. When Postmaster General John Wanamaker, a fan of

OWNEY THE DOG: US POSTAL MASCOT AT THE NATIONAL POSTAL MUSEUM

WHAT: An abandoned dog who became the unofficial mascot of the US Postal System and is honored in the National Postal Museum

WHERE: Smithsonian National Postal Museum: 2 Massachusetts Ave. NE, Washington, DC

COST: Free

PRO TIP: A song telling Owney's story can be heard on the Postal Museum's website. The music was written by Stephen Michael Schwart and sung by country singer Trace Atkins. postalmuseum.si.edu

Left: *US mail clerks and Owney, the unofficial mascot of the US Postal System, take time to pose during one of their many cross-country trips.* Right: *Owney adorned with numerous medals and tags to honor his extensive travels. Photos courtesy of the National Postal Museum, Smithsonian Institution.*

Owney's, discovered that Owney's collar was weighed down by the accumulating tags, he gave Owney a vest where postal workers could pin his extensive tag collection.

In 1897, a postal worker in Toledo, Ohio, invited a local newspaper reporter to see Owney, who was chained in the post office basement. The barking dog appeared anxious and bit the postal worker on the hand. News about the postal worker's injury and Owney's agitated behavior circulated. The Toledo postmaster called for a police officer to shoot Owney, terminating the beloved dog's career as the famed canine postal assistant.

Following Owney's tragic death, mail clerks raised money to have him preserved and he was given to the Post Office Department's Headquarters in DC. In 1911, the cherished dog was transferred to the Smithsonian Institute, where he's remained ever since. Visitors can see Owney in the National Postal Museum's atrium, clad in his famous vest, surrounded by several of his tags.

Owney made an around-the-world trip in 1895. He traveled with mailbags on trains across Europe and aboard steamships to Asia before returning to Albany, New York.

CALLING ALL STOMACHS OF STEEL

Where can you see the bullet that killed President Lincoln, a massive stomach-shaped hairball, and an elephantiasis leg?

Washington, DC, is host to an incredible wealth of museums, housing everything from national treasures, famous paintings, and historical artifacts. While museums belonging to the world-renowned Smithsonian conglomerate often receive the most acclaim and visitors, there are a plethora of smaller and lesser-known museums also deserving of attention and time. The fascinating and quirky National Museum of Health and Medicine is undoubtedly one of them.

Founded at the start of the Civil War, the museum was created to further the research of military field surgery. Surgeon General William Hammond commanded Union doctors on the battlefield to send him "specimens of morbid anatomy . . . together with projectiles and foreign bodies removed." The Army Medical Museum (the museum's original name) was led by doctors, and it quickly acquired a bevy of gruesome artifacts for the staff to examine on their way to the front. While the museum is no longer run by medical doctors, exhibits depicting the history of military medicine continue to be a mainstay. These exhibits, along with a number of medical specimens, continue to attract visitors each year.

So, what are some of the grisly items on display? A few of the main attractions include a conjoined twin specimen preserved in alcohol, a human hairball that was removed from a 12-year-old girl

---

The museum was originally housed behind the Walter Reed Army Medical Center before moving to its present location in Silver Spring, Maryland.

A look inside the unusual and sometimes unsettling National Museum of Health and Medicine. Photo courtesy of Otis Historical Archives via Creative Commons.

NATIONAL MUSEUM OF HEALTH AND MEDICINE

WHAT: A museum dedicated to the history of military medicine as well as medical oddities and specimens of morbid anatomy

WHERE: 2500 Linden Ln., Silver Spring, MD

COST: Free

PRO TIP: Open daily from 10 a.m. to 5:30 p.m. Closed December 25. The nearest metro station is Forest Glen, which is approximately 1 mile away.

who compulsively ate her hair for six years, a giant megacolon, an elephantiasis leg, and a row of skeletons ordered by height representing different stages of development. Perhaps the museum's greatest draw, however, is bone fragments and hair from President Abraham's Lincoln's skull along with the bullet that ultimately killed him. This unique and arguably bizarre museum is a treasure trove for anyone curious about medical oddities, diseases, and science. Just make sure you arrive on an empty stomach.

BALD-HEADED AND A LITTLE BIT OF COMFORT

How did sketches of a big-nosed, bald man provide comfort to soldiers around the world?

Wandering around the World War II Memorial evokes numerous emotions: feelings of sorrow, honor, remembrance, and respect, just to name a few. Individuals walking near the Pennsylvania pillar, however, may find themselves feeling additional emotions of surprise and bewilderment.

During World War II, various drawings of a large-nosed, bald man peering over a fence next to the words, "Kilroy was here" popped up all over the globe wherever battles were being fought. The mysterious sketches were proof that an American comrade had previously been there, providing comfort and reassurance to many anxious soldiers. The identity of the artist behind the graffiti was unknown, resulting in many to be confused by these peculiar drawings, including German and Japanese troops. It is said that even Adolf Hitler sought out to uncover the reason and individual(s) responsible for the sketches, as he eventually determined the culprit to be a cunning spy.

One of Kilroy's boldest appearances was at the Potsdam Conference in 1945. During the conference, President Harry Truman, Winston Churchill, and Joseph Stalin had private access to a VIP

"KILROY WAS HERE" GRAFFITI AT THE WORLD WAR II MEMORIAL

WHAT: Drawings of a big-nosed, bald man sketched around the world where battles were fought used to provide comfort to frightened soldiers

WHERE: 1750 Independence Ave. SW, Washington, DC

COST: Free

PRO TIP: The "Kilroy Was Here" graffiti sketch is located behind the golden gate next to the Pennsylvania pillar.

Top: *The grand and moving World War II Memorial. Photo courtesy of Washington.org.* Inset: *"Kilroy Was Here" graffiti sketch somewhat hidden behind the golden gate next to the Pennsylvania pillar. Photo courtesy of Luis Rubio from Alexandria, VA, USA via Creative Commons.*

restroom. One day, Stalin allegedly used the bathroom and came out demanding to know who Kilroy was, having seen the puzzling drawing on one of the bathroom walls.

While the popularity surrounding 'Kilroy was here" eventually dwindled, the widely recognized graffiti symbol can still be seen around the world, causing some to fondly remember its historical meaning and others to scratch their own heads in bemusement.

The rock band Styx named their eleventh album Kilroy Was Here after the famous World War II graffiti.

TO THE MOON AND BACK

How did a piece of the moon end up in one of the Washington National Cathedral's windows?

As the sixth largest cathedral in the world and the second largest in the United States, the Washington National Cathedral could be described as other-worldly. Perhaps no other feature further confirms this bold description than the fact that there is a small fragment of the moon in one of its windows, thanks to the three men who were the first to ever set foot on the moon. Five years after Apollo 11 astronauts Michael Collins, Neil Armstrong, and Edwin "Buzz" Aldrin made history, they personally delivered the seven-gram sample of stone to the cathedral on July 21, 1974.

In the four years leading up to the lunar rock arriving at the cathedral, NASA administrator Dr. Thomas Pain collaborated with St. Louis artist Rodney Winfield to design and build the window that contained the rock. The other-worldly stained glass, frequently dubbed the Space Window, portrays stars and orbiting planets in brilliant colors of blue, green, white, red, and orange. The vibrant creation was modeled after photos taken during the Apollo 11 mission.

The rock was painstakingly installed between two pieces of glass in the upper half of the window. The sample was sealed in a compact, airtight, nitrogen-filled environment to prevent air from entering in, which would ultimately cause deterioration. The 3.6-billion-year-old lunar rock that Armstrong and Aldrin collected is tiny, weighing a scant 7.18 grams, similar to the weight of a standard pencil. It was gathered from the Moon's Sea of

---

The West Rose window, another prominent window of the cathedral, contains over 10,500 pieces of glass.

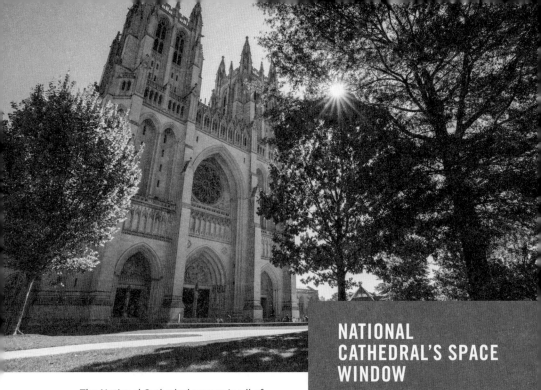

The National Cathedral towers in all of their grandeur and glory. Photo courtesy of Washington National Cathedral.

Tranquility and is primarily made of basalt, believed to be derived from lava flow. Pyroxferroite, a mineral unknown on Earth and one of the three minerals discovered on the moon, was also found in the rock.

SPRUCING THINGS UP WITH SOME CHAINSAW SCULPTURES

What was the inspiration behind the wooden chainsaw sculptures at Glenwood Cemetery?

Since 1852, Glenwood Cemetery, a historically private and secular cemetery, has been characterized by elaborate Victorian monuments and its notorious residents. It is the final resting place of George Atzerodt, a co-conspirator in Abraham Lincoln's assassination, and the infamous murderer Frederic De Frouville. More recently, however, the countless graves have been joined by less typical cemetery inhabitants: towering intricately carved wooden sculptures emerging out of the ground.

Faced with many aging and dead trees, along with those severely damaged in heavy storms, Glenwood Cemetery decided to turn an eyesore into creative art. The cemetery contacted a professional chainsaw artist, Dayton Scoggins, to transform the deteriorating trees into unique wooden sculptures. Inspired by passages in the Bible's Book of Revelation, Scoggins used four large oak trees to carve the soaring sculptures.

The four wooden carvings are as unique as they are out of place. The largest sculpture, towering 30 feet tall, depicts a massive dragon's arm catching a smaller dragon. Next to the dragon is a piece

---

CHAINSAW SCULPTURES AT GLENWOOD CEMETERY

WHAT: Towering unified wooden sculptures that were created to transform dead or dying trees into works of art

WHERE: 2219 Lincoln Rd. NE, Washington, DC

COST: Free

PRO TIP: The sculptures are situated behind the cemetery's Romanesque mortuary chapel.

Left: *An angelic wooden sculpture holding the chains that hold the dragon captive.* Right: *The largest of the four wooden sculptures depicts an enormous dragon's arm catching a smaller dragon. Photos courtesy of The Glenwood Cemetery.*

showing a sabertooth tiger with woodland animals at its feet. The other two sculptures represent angels, one standing on a column with its wings spread wide, and the other holding the chains that bind the dragon.

The unconventional chainsaw sculptures have slowly developed into a minor tourist attraction in their own right.

It's believed that the earliest chainsaw carvings date back to the 1950s, when a young man named Ray Murphy used a chainsaw to spell out his brother's name in a piece of wood.

THE MUSHROOM HOUSE

What's the story behind one of the most strangely designed homes in the Washington, DC, area?

The charming city of Bethesda, Maryland has been consistently ranked as one of the country's most affluent communities. Palatial residences with matching hefty price tags are pretty much par for the course throughout this attractive DC suburb. There's one estate, however, that's not quite like its neighbors. Not only does the peculiar estate stick out like a massive sore thumb, but it looks more like the movie set of *Alice in Wonderland* than a place one would call home. The "Mushroom House" is one of the most bizarrely designed homes in the entire DC metro region.

The famous Mushroom House was built in 1923 by its initial owners, Edward and Frances Garfinkle. Fifty years later, the couple enlisted architect Roy Mason to remodel the home, resulting in a whimsical structure characterized by 30-foot ceilings and distinctive arches and curves. The home's unusual, curvy shape helped earn its fungus nickname. In 2015 the home was purchased by Brian Vaughn, who renovated the basement, restored the kitchen and laundry rooms, and refurbished the exterior by applying fresh coats of paint and a new polyurethane shell. Vaughn also removed a number of trees from the property and filled the closed-off openings with cutouts from the removed trees. A sign labeled "The Shroom" is prominently displayed on the front of the fantastical home.

The Mushroom's interior is equally appealing. The 5,500 square foot home features six bedrooms, five bathrooms, multiple skylights, an eye-catching bar and loft, and unique woodwork and

---

The Mushroom House has also been nicknamed the "Flintstone House" and the "Smurf House."

The eccentric and wildly intriguing Bethesda home that's been dubbed the "Mushroom House." Photo courtesy of Kathryn Stansbery.

accents. In September 2018, the Mushroom House sold for $1,520,000. While the Mushroom House may not be for everyone, and it's most likely the talk of the neighborhood, it's been simultaneously fascinating and perplexing neighbors and visitors for decades and won't stop doing so anytime soon.

THE MUSHROOM HOUSE

WHAT: An unusual home that is shaped like a mushroom and characterized by numerous arches and curves

WHERE: 4949 Allan Rd., Bethesda, MD

COST: Free for those who wish to drive by or stroll throughout the neighborhood

PRO TIP: The Mushroom House sits less than a block from the DC/Maryland line.

PROST! A BREWMASTER AND HIS CASTLE (page 130)

HOFF THE HARMONICA CASE MAN (page 168)

ROLL WITH IT: THE PLOTTING OF A
PRESIDENTIAL ASSASSINATION (page 156)

HINDU GODDESS AND PRESIDENT BARACK OBAMA (page 106)

OOPS! WE DIDN'T MEAN TO SHOOT, MR. PRESIDENT! (page 186)

ONE TOUGH TREE (page 54)

ON THE STRAIGHT AND NARROW, IN SPITE OF IT ALL (page 110)

BALD-HEADED AND A LITTLE BIT OF COMFORT (page 80)

TO THE MOON AND BACK (page 82)

STAIRWAY TO CREEPINESS (page 6)

THE MIXED-UP FILES OF THE UNDERGROUND (page 174)

A FAIRYLAND TO CALL HOME (page 16)

KEEP IT IN THE VAULT (page 36)

HINDU GODDESS AND PRESIDENT BARACK OBAMA

How did one embassy choose to express their love and admiration for the United States and President Barack Obama?

Expressions of respect, love, and admiration can come in many forms. In a city like Washington, DC, it's not uncommon for that type of expression to come in an overt form, like by erecting a monument or statue. The Indonesian Embassy chose to do just that when they unveiled a statue of Saraswati, the epochal Hindu representation of education, on their grounds, simultaneously declaring their partnership with the United States while expressing their adoration of the United States' 44th president.

Saraswati is the Hindu goddess of knowledge, love, wisdom, arts, music and learning. The idea of the sculpture came from Indonesian Ambassador Dr. Dino Patti Djalal and it was built with the assistance of the National Economic Committee and Bali's Badung Regent. The predominantly white statue stands 16 feet tall and features gold accents. The Goddess has four arms. Her front left hand plays a musical instrument, her back right hand holds a manuscript symbolizing knowledge, and her back-left hand holds akshamala, or prayer beads, which represent the continuous process of learning. The centerpiece is a sizeable swan, reminding onlookers the difference between right and wrong. Arguably the most notable

SARASWATI STATUE

WHAT: A statue of the epochal Hindu Goddess of art and education that includes a young Barack Obama reading a book

WHERE: Embassy of Indonesia: 2020 Massachusetts Ave. NW, Washington, DC

COST: Free

PRO TIP: The Embassy of Indonesia is closed during Indonesian and US holidays.

Left: *The Hindu goddess of art and education statue towering over a young Barack Obama reading with his classmates. Photo courtesy of AgnosticPreachersKid via Creative Commons.* Right: *Embassy of Indonesia located on the prestigious Embassy Row. Photo courtesy of Robert Bolton via Creative Commons.*

part of the statue is the three young children sitting at its base reading a book. The child seated on the left is a young Barack Obama, who lived in Indonesia from ages six to ten. The sculpture depicts Obama reading with his classmates during his time in grade school in Indonesia.

When asked to describe the cultural gift, a spokesperson of the Indonesian Embassy stated, "Her representation at the Indonesian Embassy was not decided out only of any religious grounds, but more on its symbolized values that parallel with several key principles of Indonesia—US relations under comprehensive partnership, in particular education and people-to-people contact." The majestic statue stands on top of a lotus in front of the Indonesian Embassy a block from the Indian embassy and a mile from the White House.

In December 2009, a statue of Barack Obama as a 10-year-old was installed in Jakarta's Menteng Park to inspire children in Indonesia. After public backlash, it was removed and relocated to the former president's school in Jakarta.

RAISING CANE

Why was a Massachusetts senator brutally beaten by a congressman?

Washington is no stranger to political discourse. Often debates become heated, rivalries are established, and individuals are sometimes demonized more than they are persuaded. Arguments erupting on the House Floor and Senate Chamber have become commonplace. On May 22, 1856, however, the familiar combative banter turned violent when a member of the House of Representatives entered the Senate Chamber and bludgeoned a senator into unconsciousness.

Three days prior to the egregious attack, Massachusetts Senator Charles Sumner, an antislavery Republican, delivered a passionate speech entitled "Crime Against Kansas" on the controversial issue of whether Kansas should be admitted to the Union as a slave state or free state. Sumner criticized two Democrat senators, Stephen Douglas of Illinois and Andrew Butler of South Carolina. He spewed a plethora of insults, calling Douglas a "noise-some, squat, and nameless animal...not a proper model for an American senator" and accusing Butler, who was not present, of taking "a mistress . . . who, though ugly to others, is always lovely to him; though polluted in the sight of the world, is chaste in his sight—I mean, the harlot, Slavery."

Representative Preston Brooks, who was present for Sumner's abrasive insolence, was a distant cousin of Butler.

Immediately after the violent incident, Butler was hailed a hero and South Carolina held events in his honor. Southerners from across the region sent Butler replacement canes, which outraged northerners even more than the caning itself.

The mighty dome of the US Capitol weighing a whopping 4,500 tons. Photo courtesy of the Carol M. Highsmith Archive, Library of Congress, Prints and Photographs Division.

THE CANING OF SENATOR CHARLES SUMNER

WHAT: A brutal attack by Congressman Andrew Butler on Senator Charles Sumner in response to a fiery anti-slavery speech characterized by aggressive insults

WHERE: US Capitol: First St. SE, Washington, DC

COST: Public tours of the US Capitol are free; Each tour is walk-up only and limited to 50 visitors.

PRO TIP: Guides using translation devices lead foreign tours each day. Tours in Mandarin and Spanish are offered at 8:40 a.m.

Defending his family's reputation, he entered the chamber after the Senate adjourned and brutally struck an unsuspecting Sumner over the head with a metal-topped cane. While Brooks repeatedly walloped Sumner with his cane, Sumner rose and stumbled around the chamber, unsuccessfully trying to protect himself. After a long minute, the attack finally ended. The cane shattered from the incessant blows.

A bloodied and battered Sumner was carried away, while Brooks calmly walked out of the chamber without being detained. Brooks resigned, was immediately reelected, and died soon after at the age of 37. Sumner slowly recovered and returned to the Senate, where he served eighteen more years. Voters of Massachusetts reelected Sumner and let his seat sit vacant during his absence as a reminder of Southern brutality.

ON THE STRAIGHT AND NARROW, IN SPITE OF IT ALL

What was the inspiration behind the narrowest house in America?

Many individuals living in the Washington, DC, area have grown accustomed to living in small spaces. Washingtonians have learned to become quite savvy at consolidating, arranging, and cramming their belongings into compact spaces. But even the most adept consolidators' skills would be tested in Alexandria's Spite House, the narrowest house in America. At seven feet wide and approximately 25 feet deep, the bright blue Spite House, as it's often called, has been identified as the country's narrowest house. It spans two stories and measures a mere 325 square feet. This cozy structure may look adorable and welcoming, but its origins prove quite the contrary.

In 1830, John Hollensbury, the owner of one of the adjacent houses, built the house to keep horse-drawn wagons and loiterers out of his alley. Hollensbury, a city council member and a bricklayer, was fed up with the raucous alleyway shenanigans and numerous pockmarks on the side of his home due to wagon collisions. He decided to take matters in his own hands and began laying bricks to close off the alleyway. Two facing walls and a roof later, Hollensbury had succeeded in blocking off the alleyway by adding an addition to his home.

Whether Hollensbury had an actual permit or used his power as a councilmember is still unknown. Due to the power of the Ex

HOLLENSBURY SPITE HOUSE

WHAT: The narrowest house in America, motivated by spite.

WHERE: 523 Queen St., Alexandria, VA

COST: Free for passersby strolling along the cobble-stoned streets of Alexandria

PRO TIP: The Hollensbury House is located in Alexandria's Old Town district.

The Hollensbury Spite House, America's narrowest home, motivated by spite. Photo courtesy of Dena Palamedes.

Post Facto law, which states that the consequences of breaking a law cannot be applied for actions taken before the law was enacted, the Spite House is exempt from the criteria of DC's modern-day building code. In 1990, the Sammis family purchased the home for $135,000 and has owned it ever since. They do not live here full-time, as they prefer to use the Spite House as their "pied-a-terre."

Ripley's Believe it or Not nicknamed the Spite House "The narrowest house in America."

WHEN THREE AND A HALF MINUTES FEELS LIKE AN ETERNITY

Where can you find the western hemisphere's longest set of single-span escalators?

Commuters traveling via the Wheaton Metrorail station, located right outside of the District in Maryland's Montgomery County, will need to add a few more minutes to their morning and evening commutes if they plan on riding the metro's escalator. Three and a half more minutes to be exact.

The Western Hemisphere's longest set of single-span escalators can be found along the metro's red line, spanning the length of two football fields. Ascending from the deep hollow of Wheaton's metro to street level will take riders a whopping three and half minutes. While that may not seem like a significant amount of time in the grand scheme of things, it's worth asking yourself, when was the last time you rode on an escalator for longer than a minute, or even two minutes? Most likely, not often. Unless, that is, you are a frequent commuter on the Wheaton metro stop.

The Wheaton metro station is not the only Washington metro station of impressive magnitude. The Forest Glen station, which precedes the Wheaton station along the red line, is the

WHEATON METRO STATION

WHAT: A Washington metro station that is home to the western hemisphere's longest set of single-span escalators

WHERE: 11171 Georgia Ave., Silver Spring, MD

COST: While riding the escalator is free, metro fares vary upon starting point and destination

PRO TIP: The metro opens at 5 a.m. during the week and at 7 a.m. on the weekends. It closes for several hours each night.

The Wheaton metro station's never-ending escalators. Photo courtesy of Bohemian Baltimore.

metro system's deepest station. Situated a staggering 196 feet underground, the station has replaced escalators with high-speed elevators in transporting passengers to and from the surface. Wheaton station trails behind Forest Glen as the second deepest station of Washington's extensive system.

The escalator's 230-foot moving staircase travels at a speed of 90 feet per minute.

THE TRUTH SHALL SET YOU FREELY TALKING

How did one of America's first psychiatric hospitals get involved with interrogating Nazi prisoners of war?

Perched atop an isolated hilltop in Southeast Washington, DC, Saint Elizabeths Hospital has been regarded as a pioneer in the treatment of mental illness since its opening in 1855 as one of America's first psychiatric hospitals. Its notoriety is not without controversy, however, as the famous asylum is also known for its controversial involvement in wartime interrogations.

In 1942, Saint Elizabeths partnered with the proto-CIA Office of Strategic Services (OSS) to assist in prisoner of war interrogations. The hospital's director and superintendent Dr. Winfred Overholser began to study marijuana as a truth serum in efforts to force Nazis to reveal intel to interrogators to help win World War II. Three types of cannabis were explored: cannabinol from Indian charas, tetrahydrocannabinol acetate, and synthetic cannabinol. The acetate derivative was found to be the most effective.

The OSS's research led to a procedure for injecting small amounts of THC acetate into cigarettes with hypodermic needles. These spiked cigarettes were slowly disseminated to test subjects throughout 60-minute sessions, resulting in individuals becoming more animated, and speaking more freely and without discretion.

SAINT ELIZABETHS HOSPITAL

WHAT: One of America's first psychiatric hospitals, which aided the government's prisoner of war interrogations during World War II

WHERE: 1100 Alabama Ave. SE, Washington, DC

COST: Free for those listed on a patient's visitor's list

PRO TIP: Visitors to the hospital must be on a patient's visitors list.

Top left: *The once-distinguished Saint Elizabeths Hospital that was a trailblazer in psychiatric care.* Top and bottom right: *A look inside the pristine and well-maintained Saint Elizabeths Hospital, before its controversial and inhumane treatment practices tarnished its reputation forever. Photos courtesy of the Library of Congress.*

Only one year later, these truth serum experiments ended in 1943, with the government deducing that the use of marijuana was not amenable for sustained interrogation. While Saint Elizabeths' complicity in wartime interrogations occupied only a brief stint in its longtime history, this problematic collaboration is not its only blemish. Throughout the years, the hospital has also performed invalidated electroshock therapy and forced lobotomization.

Today much of Saint Elizabeths is vacant, slated for major renovation as a new Department of Homeland Security facility.

Saint Elizabeths was originally named the Government Hospital for the Insane.

A PENNY FOR YOUR THOUGHTS: ACTUALLY, MAKE THAT 10,000

Why did one DC couple choose to create a map of the District out of 10,000 pennies to adorn their shower wall?

Washington, DC, is known as a transient city, but many of those who have come here have ultimately embraced it as their adopted home. Regardless of their origins, Washingtonians tend to be a proud and vocal group, often eager to share their pride and enthusiasm for the capital city that they now call home.

Perhaps no place exemplifies DC pride more than in the Eckington home of transplant couple Andrea Peterson and Matt Separa. Committed to combatting the pervasive cookie-cutter theme characterizing many DC homes, Peterson and Separa fought back by personalizing their home renovation. They chose to construct a giant map of the city they've called home for over a decade in their shower stall using approximately 10,000 pennies.

The elaborate project took several months to complete, starting with Peterson obtaining four $25 boxes of rolled up pennies from the bank. Next, she organized the pennies by color and sheen, laboriously cleaning and polishing numerous tarnished pennies. At the same time, she didn't want all of the pennies to look brand-new. She wanted to incorporate her love for the water and kayaking by showcasing DC's waterways on the penny-tiled map. The couple achieved this effect by using patina acrylic paint to enhance the bluish tint of these specific pennies. The large design was mounted on drywall by using Gorilla Glue to affix the pennies into place.

A special silver penny is embedded into the penny-tiled map, marking the location of the couple's Eckington home.

A shower-wall map of the District of Columbia made up entirely of pennies. 10,000 if you're keeping count. Photo courtesy of JoAnn Hill.

Finally, the penny masterpiece was grouted, similar to normal tiling, and sealed with epoxy and six coats of acrylic paint.

The couple's shower stall isn't the only place in the house that is adorned with pennies. A penny-designed portrait of abolitionist John Brown, along with various copper-themed accents, are tastefully dispersed throughout the meticulously designed home.

THE 10,000 PENNY SHOWER STALL MAP OF WASHINGTON, DC

WHAT: A giant DC map constructed of 10,000 pennies in a couple's shower stall

WHERE: 124 Todd Place NE, Washington, DC

COST: This is a private residence and not open for tours.

PRO TIP: The Eckington couple is considering renting out the part of their home that includes the unique penny-tiled shower map on Airbnb in the near future.

A SPY AND A SOVIET WALK INTO A BAR

How is a long-time Georgetown haunt linked to one of the country's biggest betrayals in history?

Those looking to grab a beer or nosh on some casual pub fare at Georgetown's popular Mr. Smith's restaurant and bar may be surprised to hear that this long-standing institution once played a major role in DC's spy scene. The former home of Chadwicks, a long-time Georgetown favorite, was once the setting of one of the biggest betrayals in our country's history.

On June 13, 1985, CIA counterintelligence officer Aldrich Ames met with Soviet chief Vikto Cherkashin at the restaurant, where he purportedly divulged the names of over 100 CIA agents working undercover in the Soviet Union. Fluent in Russian, Ames was burdened with financial problems, and in addition he held the Soviet Union in high esteem. Both matters ultimately led to Ames disclosing the identities of undercover CIA operatives by jotting their names down on a notepad. The risky act of betrayal came with a hefty payout of $4.6 million. Ames' sudden windfall, however, did not go unnoticed, as he began recklessly spending his new fortune on luxurious items. Many began to question how his $60,000 salary could possibly fund the $500,000 home he bought in cash, the luxury Jaguar car

ESPIONAGE BETRAYAL AT GEORGETOWN'S FORMER CHADWICKS RESTAURANT

WHAT: The popular eatery where a CIA agent divulged the names of over 100 CIA agents working undercover in the Soviet Union

WHERE: 3205 Water St. NW, Washington, DC

COST: Dependent upon how much food and drink you order

PRO TIP: Chadwicks has since been replaced by Mr. Smith's of Georgetown, a popular and convivial neighborhood restaurant and bar.

Mr. Smith's, the popular Georgetown restaurant and bar where a CIA agent once divulged the names of over 100 CIA agents working undercover in the Soviet Union. Photos courtesy of Mr. Smith's.

he drove, and expensive tailored suits he wore to work. The CIA became increasingly alarmed once agents began disappearing in the field and executions were carried out. They eventually linked Ames' unexplained wealth with these egregious acts, arrested him, and charged him with espionage acts.

Aldrich Ames pleaded guilty and was sentenced to incarceration for life without the possibility of parole. He is serving his life sentence in the federal prison system. Ames' wife, Rosario Ames, served a 63-month prison sentence for aiding and abetting Ames' espionage activities.

In accordance to Aldrich Ames' plea agreement, he relinquished his assets to the United States, and $547,000 was handed over to the Justice Department's Victims Assistance Fund.

ART IMITATES LIFE AND GO-GO PLAYS ON

Which DC memorial can be played as a musical instrument while paying tribute to the city's official music and its beloved creator?

After being considered the unofficial music of Washington, DC, for nearly 50 years, Go-Go was finally declared the official sound of the nation's capital in February 2020. Since its inception in the early 1970s, the drum-based fusion of funk, hip hop, R&B, and blues has been influenced by many artists including Rare Essence, Trouble Funk, and Junkyard Band. None, however, have had a greater impact on Go-Go than born-and-bred Washingtonian Chuck Brown. The legendary godfather of Go-Go is credited with creating the genre and helping embed it into the cultural fabric of Washington, DC.

The Go-Go pioneer is so beloved that on August 22, 2014, which would have been his 78th birthday, the city dedicated a section of Langdon Park to the artist, naming it Chuck Brown Memorial Park. A 16-foot-tall abstract art sculpture, named "Wind Me Up, Chuck" by local sculptor and creator Jackie Braitman, was installed near the park's entrance. The unique art structure stands near the park's playground and includes colorful instruments for children complete with interactive pulsing lights aligned to funky beats and percussive instruments just begging to be played. Displayed near the art installation is a mosaic retaining wall chronicling 10 moments and images from Brown's vibrant life.

Chuck Brown's biggest hit, "Bustin' Loose," was sampled on Nelly's "Hot in Herre," and it was also used in a Chips Ahoy commercial in 2010.

The park's mosaic retaining wall chronicling 10 moments and images from Chuck Brown's vibrant life. Photo courtesy of S Pakhrin from DC, USA via Creative Commons.

The city's love for the Go-Go icon extends far beyond the memorial and park. Several murals throughout the district vibrantly feature the revered star and the street at the 1900 block of 7th Street NW where it crosses with Florida Avenue NW has been named Chuck Brown Way.

CHUCK BROWN MEMORIAL

WHAT: A musically interactive art memorial honoring DC's late Go-Go legend Chuck Brown

WHERE: Chuck Brown Memorial Park, 2901 20th St. NE, Washington, DC

COST: Free

PRO TIP: Fans and residents come together every August 22nd to honor the late musician for Chuck Brown Day.

THE APPLE DOESN'T FALL FAR FROM THE TREE

Which heavily guarded tree serves as a living tribute to one of the world's most prestigious scientists in history?

A plaque reading, "Science has its traditions, as well as its frontiers," prominently sits among a group of embassies on the former National Bureau of Standards (NBS) campus, paying tribute to one of the most revered and influential scientists in history, Sir Isaac Newton. One tree in this collection, however, stands out among the rest. A clone of Newton's infamous apple tree stands proudly, honoring Newton's theory of gravity.

The original apple tree, known for centuries as the source of an apple that fell and hit Newton on the head, thus leading to the discovery of the law of gravity, remains on the estate of his former home. Newton's Woolsthorpe Manor, located in the county of Lincolnshire, England, continues to serve as a reminder of his numerous contributions to science. Irvine C. Gardner, an NBS scientist, obtained four cuttings from the hallowed trunk and proceeded to plant one of the clones near the NBS in 1957. The study of gravity has been integral to the NBS' work, and the apple-tree clone has become a treasured tribute to Newton's invaluable discoveries in this branch of science.

NIST NEWTON APPLE TREE

WHAT: A clone of the famous apple tree that supposedly led to Sir Isaac Newton discovering the law of gravity

WHERE: International Park, Washington, DC; Northwest of Cleveland Park

COST: Free

PRO TIP: Although the president's security detail may guard this tree, visitors can still walk right up to witness it in all of its brilliant blooming glory.

The clone of Sir Isaac Newton's infamous apple tree extends its branches across the lawn of the National Institute of Standards and Technology. Photo courtesy of Stoughton/NIST.

The Bureau has relocated to Gaithersburg, Maryland and has since changed its name to the National Institute of Standards and Technology (NIST). Not to worry though; the famous Newton tree is under the care of some of the most carefully trained individuals on the planet. The US Secret Service has been assigned to overseeing the protection of the sacred specimen, making it one particularly safely guarded tree.

Newton's cloned tree died in the late 1990s; however, another cutting had already been preserved. A clone of the clone was planted in 2000 and continues to thrive.

PET CEMETERY: A FINAL BURIAL PLACE FOR BELOVED PETS

Where are over 50,000 pets along with 58 humans buried right outside the country's capital city?

Mention the words "pet cemetery" and there's a good chance that many will conjure up gruesome and alarming images from Stephen King's famous horror film. Real-life pet cemeteries, however, offer a much more peaceful experience. Aspin Hill Pet Cemetery is located just a few minutes outside of Washington, DC, and serves as a burial place not only for a wide array of beloved pets, but in some cases for their owners, too.

Commissioned by the Maryland's Montgomery County Humane Society, Silver Spring's Aspin Hill Pet Cemetery was founded in 1920 when dog breeders Richard and Bertha Birney purchased eight acres of land to build a kennel to breed dogs. In the beginning, the Birneys used the land to bury their dogs as well as the dogs of their close friends. As the kennel grew and word began to spread, others wanted a place of rest for their beloved pets, too. Initially, the graves were small and plainly marked stones engraved with the animals' and families' names and relevant dates. Eventually, the graves became more intricately designed, incorporating large statues, ornate rock walls, and even a mausoleum for a highly revered dog named Mickey. The cemetery

Several of FBI director J. Edgar Hoover's dogs are buried in Aspin Hill, as is Rags, the decorated dog-mascot of the 1st Infantry Division who delivered a crucial message that saved lives in World War I.

MOSES

1986 1999

DOG CHERISHED FRIEND
ALWAYS LOVED
FOREVER MISSED

Remembering Moses, a cherished and beloved friend. Photo courtesy of Montgomery County Humane Society.

ASPIN HILL PET CEMETERY

WHAT: The country's second-oldest pet cemetery that's home to over 50,000 pets and 58 humans.

WHERE: 13630 Georgia Ave., Silver Spring, MD

COST: Free

PRO TIP: The cemetery is open from dusk to dawn.

has also evolved as a burial place well beyond dogs and cats. Birds, goats, monkeys, frogs, hamsters, turtles, snakes, and goldfish, among other animals, have all been buried here. In addition, 58 humans have been laid to rest here as well.

Aspin Hill is not currently selling plots because of limited space; only present owners who have available space can bury their pets at this time. The Montgomery County Humane Society is currently working on rehabilitating the cemetery's grounds and buildings and hopes to offer future programs on animal welfare.

THE WORLD'S MOST DANGEROUS HOT DOG STAND

How did one hot dog stand end up being a prime target during the Cold War?

Many of us realize that eating too many hot dogs can lead to a number of health problems, but did you know that for nearly three decades, those who chose to eat them from a particular cart in the Pentagon faced another paramount danger, far beyond the typical health concerns?

Throughout much of the Cold War, no less than two Soviet missiles were aimed at the small hot dog cart that stood in the Pentagon's center courtyard. The Soviets were under the impression that the cart was the Pentagon's most secretive meeting spot, and the entire building was a large compound built around it. The Soviets were using satellite imagery to monitor the groups of US military officers visiting the stand and believed that the stand served as an entrance to an underground bunker. They thought that officers were going there to obtain top-secret briefings in this discreet area. Little did they know that these individuals were simply coming to grab some lunch. Tour guides have been known to tell their tour groups, "This is where the building earned the nickname Cafe Ground Zero, the deadliest hot dog stand in the world."

PENTAGON HOT DOG STAND

WHAT: The site of the Pentagon's former hot dog stand that Russians believed served as a secretive meeting spot during the Cold War

WHERE: The Pentagon, Arlington, VA

COST: Free

PRO TIP: All guided tours of the Pentagon are free and available by reservation only. Tours are conducted Monday through Thursday from 10 a.m. to 4 p.m. and Friday from noon to 4 p.m.

Standing at the center of the courtyard of the Pentagon is the unassuming hot dog stand widely known as Cafe Ground Zero. Photo courtesy of Steven Donald Smith.

The missile-targeted hot dog stand was torn down in 2006 and replaced with a more modern food court that Pentagon employees can visit year-round. Because the Pentagon was identified as a national historic landmark in 1992 and the courtyard is one of the five historically protected locations of the complex, the hot dog stand had to be replaced by a structure of approximately the same size and precisely the same shape as the original.

Russian officials have never confirmed that they aimed at least two missiles at the Pentagon's hot dog stand for nearly 30 years.

UNDER HIS EYE

Why is there a creepy mannequin keeping watch over Old Town Alexandria?

If you've spent time strolling through Old Town Alexandria's quaint cobble-stone streets, then you may have noticed an eerie mannequin lurking in an attic visible from Pendleton Street. The wax figure is much more than just a creepy lurker. There's a fascinating story behind its history and how it's been keeping a watchful eye on the city for years.

Dubbed "Oscar," the decaying one-eyed watchman was discovered by Bud Jordan when his real estate agency began to occupy offices in the historic building in the late 1970s. He and his team found the lone figure in the attic and learned about its past. Then they dressed him in Jordan's suit, tie, and hat and furnished him with a lamp before returning him to his guard post.

As the story goes, during the Civil War, a rather lazy watchman named Michael Kiggin would patrol the streets of Alexandria, and when he became tired he would bring the mannequin to accompany him during his watch at the Mount Vernon Cotton Factory's window. One night, a perpetrator broke into the building and murdered the watchman. The killers fled and were never found, and in a botched ploy police officers tried to pretend that the watchman had survived in hopes of luring the killers back to the crime scene. Unfortunately, that never happened, as Kiggin was soon found dead on the factory grounds. A suspect by the name of William Arrington was eventually arrested but never tried, leaving the case unsolved and open to this day.

The building has been a cotton mill, hospital, military prison, bottling house, sparkplug factory, and apartment building and office space.

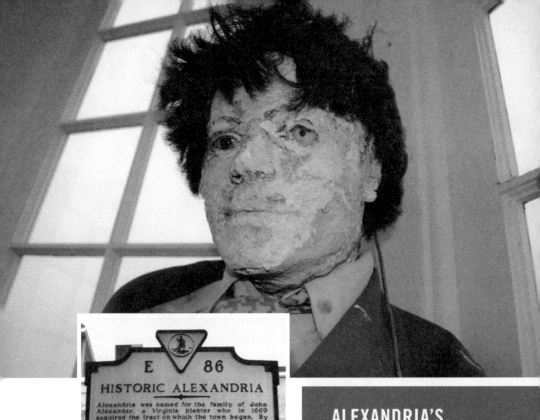

HISTORIC ALEXANDRIA

Alexandria was named for the family of John Alexander, a Virginia planter who in 1669 acquired the tract on which the town began. By 1732, the site was known as Hunting Creek Warehouse and in 1749 became Alexandria, thereafter a major 18th-century port. George Washington frequented the town; Robert E. Lee claimed it as his boyhood home. From 1801 to 1847 Alexandria was a part of the District of Columbia, and was later occupied by Federal troops during the Civil War. By the 20th century it had become a major railroad center. In 1946, Alexandria created the third historic district in the United States to protect its 18th- and 19th-century buildings.

"Oscar" the one-eyed mannequin watchman that has been looming over the streets of Alexandria, Virginia, since the Civil War. Top photo courtesy of the Alexandria Times. Inset photo courtesy of Rdmsf01 via Creative Commons.

ALEXANDRIA'S WATCHMAN MANNEQUIN

WHAT: A creepy wax mannequin that has been keeping watch over Old Town Alexandria since the Civil War

WHERE: 515 North Washington St., Alexandria, VA

COST: Free to the public

PRO TIP: Bud Jordan, the man responsible for finding and clothing the mannequin, hopes to see the watchman illuminated again, so much that he has even dropped off a box of light bulbs to speed up the process.

Today the building is quite fittingly home to the International Association of Chiefs of Police. Still clad in Bud Jordan's attire, the watchman mannequin continues to keep passersby under his eye.

PROST! A BREWMASTER AND HIS CASTLE

Why was DC's original brewery housed in an opulent castle?

DC's burgeoning craft beer and brewery scene has become a welcome mainstay of late. The art of brewing, however, is nothing new to the city. The palatial Christian Heurich House, better known as the Brewmaster's Castle, is the District's original brewery, and arguably one of the most resplendent in the nation. Situated on a tree-lined residential street in DC's affluent Dupont Circle neighborhood, the chocolate-colored castle is often overlooked by passersby. Many are unaware of its rich and fascinating history tracing back to German beer brewer Christian Heurich.

Heurich learned the art of brewing from his father as a child and immediately set out to build his beer-brewing empire upon arriving in the states in 1866. Later, in the 1890s, he built the gothic structure to be his grand palace. He created an enormous, incombustible brewery where the famous Kennedy Center stands today that could produce over half a million barrels a year. Heurich became the second largest employer in DC, surpassed only by the government. Heurich used his abundant wealth to build a palatial home with his second wife. The imposing Victorian home served as his home until his death in 1945 at the age of 102.

BREWMASTER'S CASTLE

WHAT: Dupont Circle's Heurich House Museum, also known as the Brewmaster's Castle, was DC's original beer brewery

WHERE: 1307 New Hampshire Ave. NW, Washington, DC

COST: Requested donations of $10 per person. Cost of beer events vary.

PRO TIP: Public tours are offered on Thursdays, Fridays, and Saturdays. Times vary.

The magnificent Christian Heurich House, widely known as the Brewmaster's Castle, proudly resides in Dupont Circle. Top photo courtesy of Rhaworth via Creative Commons. Inset photo courtesy of Almonroth via Creative Commons.

THE
BREWMASTER'S
CASTLE

The Christian Heurich Brewing Company eventually closed its doors and was later demolished in 1962.

Heurich's opulent home is now a national historic landmark where individuals can tour the home's beautifully preserved first two floors. Regular beer events like Oktoberfest are offered, and monthly Brewmaster Tours allow visitors to tour the palace with a beer in hand. DC's original craft beer scene is alive and well, further enhanced by its rich history.

Christian Heurich arrived in America with $200 to his name. Through his beer-brewing brilliance, he became Washington's largest private employer.

OH, SAY CAN YOU CHEAT: AN AFFAIR TURNS DEADLY

What perilous fight did Francis Scott Key's son fatally lose?

Lafayette Square, a meticulously manicured public park, is a picturesque square where locals and tourists gather to stroll, relax, and get an up-close-and-personal view of the White House, which stands directly north of the square. Five colossal statues also inhabit the space, including that of President Andrew Jackson and four Revolutionary War heroes. Today the park offers a welcomed reprieve from the hustle and bustle of the surrounding city streets; however, its history depicts a dark and dismal past.

The park has stood for over 200 years, undergoing many changes in identity. It has been used as a racetrack, zoo, graveyard, barracks for soldiers during the War of 1812, and a slave market. The pristine park is also the site of the murder of Francis Scott Key's son, Philip Barton Key II.

On February 27, 1859, Daniel Sickles, a former New York congressman and later a prominent Union general, shot and killed the national anthem's songwriter's son after learning of an affair between the younger Key and his wife, Teresa Sickles. Philip and Teresa met at an 1857 inaugural ball for President James Buchanan. Over the next year, the two lovers engaged in a sordid affair, secretly meeting in rented apartments, on parlor sofas, and in hidden corners of the Georgetown Cemetery.

Daniel Sickles' trial didn't deter him from continuing to serve his country. After he was acquitted of murder charges, he went on to serve as a major general in the Civil War, and then eventually served one more final term in the US House of Representatives.

Lafayette Square, a lovely public square within President's Park. Photo courtesy of the National Park Service.

MURDER AT LAFAYETTE PARK

WHAT: The site where Francis Scott Key's son was murdered over an affair he was having with the wife of a former congressman

WHERE: Pennsylvania Ave. NW & 16th St. NW, Washington, DC

COST: Free

PRO TIP: The park is open 24 hours.

On the night when he would meet his fate, Key had come to the park for a tryst with Mrs. Sickles, but instead was confronted and eventually shot by her irate husband. Just before shooting Key with a pistol, Sickles declared, "Key, you scoundrel, you have dishonored my home; you must die." Sickles managed to evade a conviction and was found not guilty by reason of insanity. His acquittal was the first time that this legal defense was used successfully in the United States.

ENCHANTMENT IN A STORYBOOK FOREST

Where can adults and children escape and relive their favorite fairy tale stories?

Many of our childhoods were defined by the stories and games that we played. Fairy tales originating in ancient folklore have provided escape to labyrinthine forests, whimsical castles, and magical villages for centuries. Those looking to recapture their favorite childhood memories will be delighted to know that less than 45 minutes outside of Washington lies an enchanted forest, a storybook haven brimming with innocence, nostalgia, and magic.

In August 1955, a month after Disneyland opened, the Enchanted Forest opened its storybook park in Ellicott City, Maryland. For over 30 years, families from near and far visited the popular fairy-tale complex. Generations were captivated by the park's ability to recreate a spellbinding world filled with delight and allure. At its peak, the park welcomed over 300,000 children per summer season. As larger and more impressive entertainment complexes began to open throughout the area, the Enchanted Forest's appeal began to wane, causing the park to close in the early 1990s.

More than a decade later, nearby Clark's Elioak Farm made the decision to revive the storybook-themed park by gradually acquiring

THE ENCHANTED FOREST AT CLARK'S ELIOAK FARM

WHAT: The site of a revived storybook-themed park showcasing dozens of fairy-tale characters and scenes

WHERE: Clark's Elioak Farm, 10500 Clarksville Pike, Ellicott City, MD

COST: Admission is $7.00 per person. Add-on activities such as hayrides are available for an additional fee

PRO TIP: The farm and forest are open Tuesday through Sunday from 10 a.m. to 5 p.m.

Left: *The bold and quirky Three Bears' House.* Right: *The Old Woman's Shoe. Photos courtesy of Martha Clark.*

and reinstating a number of the forgotten fairy tale items. In 2004, much to the delight of parents and kids, they procured the Cinderella pumpkin coach. A year later, they restored a slew of other items, including Mother Goose and her gosling, Jack's beanstalk affixed with the giant at the top, multiple gingerbread men, the six mice that pulled Cinderella's coach, and the crooked house and the crooked man. In 2006, the farm focused on two major projects: moving and restoring the Old Woman's shoe and the Three Bears' house. Due to their size, both items were cut in half and carefully transported to the farm. A number of parties, including tree experts and moving companies, were involved with reassembling the structures. Over subsequent years, more items were obtained and refurbished, including Sleeping Beauty, Snow White, Little Boy Blue, and Robin Hood. Since then, the farm has further enhanced the revived forest by adding over 20 new fairy-tale characters and a newly created Enchanted Forest Pine Tree Maze.

Mark Cline, the mastermind behind Foamhenge (see page 32), helped restore the park's Humpty Dumpty and Willy the Whale.

WE'RE WAITING FOR YOU, MADAM PRESIDENT

Why is there an uncarved lump behind the Portrait Monument's three suffragists' busts?

Upon entering the imposing US Capitol Rotunda, visitors are immediately surrounded by opulence, history, and an abundance of testosterone. The majority of statues and busts in the Rotunda are primarily of presidents, including Dwight David Eisenhower, Ulysses S. Grant, and Ronald Reagan. One of the few exceptions is the prominent Portrait Monument, which proudly pays tribute to women's suffrage, honoring trailblazers Lucretia Mott, Elizabeth Cady Stanton, and Susan B. Anthony. These three remarkable women were the leading forces behind the women's movement and led the crusade for women's right to vote. While the monument to these pioneering women is impressive in its own right, perhaps its most intriguing aspect is the fact that it seems to have been intentionally left unfinished.

Towering behind the three busts is an indistinct and eye-catching uncarved block of marble—an enigma that has led to a great amount of speculation over the years. According to urban myth and many Capitol tour guides, the uncarved lump is reserved for the first female president. In recent years, many visitors have wondered if Hillary Clinton would one day hold the spot. It's been theorized that the monument's sculptor, Adelaide Johnson, purposely left the statue unfinished to symbolize that women still had a very long road to acquiring equal rights and left the uncarved block to represent

Other examples of art in the US Capitol featuring females include a painting of Pocahontas and bronze statues of Rosa Parks and Sojourner Truth.

The unfinished Portrait Monument that sits in the rotunda of the US Capitol. Photo courtesy of JoAnn Hill.

THE UNFINISHED PORTRAIT MONUMENT

WHAT: A statue commemorating women's suffrage that is believed to have been intentionally left unfinished to make room for the first woman president

WHERE: US Capitol Rotunda, First St. SE, Washington, DC

COST: Public tours of the US Capitol are free.

PRO TIP: Visitors are welcome to enter the building through the Capitol Visitor Center, located underground on the east side of the Capitol.

all other women's rights leaders, past, present, and future.

A year after white women's suffrage was finally achieved, the statue was moved underground. It was hidden in a broom closet in the basement and remained there for 75 years. In 1995, which marked the 75th anniversary of the 19th Amendment, women's groups, along with multiple female members of Congress, rallied to bring the monument out from storage. With the help of donors from across the country, funds were raised to cover the $75,000 cost of moving the statue, and it was finally relocated to the Rotunda in 1997, where it remains today. A true example of art imitating life, only time will tell whether someone will ever "complete" the monument by carving a fourth bust.

A SWORD AND ITS SORCERERS

Who keeps stealing Joan of Arc's almighty sword?

From King Arthur to Game of Thrones, the world seems to have an enduring fascination with swords, and our nation's capital is no exception. For the past 80 years or so, people have been stealing the sword from the Joan of Arc statue located in Washington, DC's Meridian Park. Are these individuals simply channelling their inner Arya Stark, or is there something more?

The towering bronze Joan of Arc statue, gifted by the French women's group Le Lyceum Societie des Femmes de France, was installed in 1922. The majestic heroine is clad in full armor, powerfully mounted atop a brawny horse, and thrusting a formidable sword into the sky. The sword measures five feet long and weighs a hefty 30 pounds, so snatching the sizeable sword out of the French saint's hand would presumably be no easy feat. Unfortunately, her daunting pose also makes her sword pretty vulnerable to theft. The imposing sword was first stolen in 1932 and eventually found in a hedge, bent but still intact.

In 1978, Joan's sword was stolen once again, when someone broke off its protruding blade. It wasn't replaced until over 30 years later, in 2011. In 2016 it was finally replaced, only to be stolen again. Congresswoman Eleanor Holmes Norton called out the National Park Service (NPS) and questioned whether the NPS could have prevented the theft. "The Park Service should be able to give Joan of

JOAN OF ARC STATUE AND HER SWORD

WHAT: The coveted sword of the Joan of Arc statue that has been stolen multiple times over the past 80 years

WHERE: Meridian Hill Park, Washington, DC

COST: Free

PRO TIP: Meridian Hill Park is open 24 hours, every day of the year.

Joan of Arc, sword in hand and fiercely perched upon her horse, ready for battle. Photos courtesy of Tim Brown.

Arc her sword back and place it so securely that kids couldn't get it out," she said.

In 2018, things drastically improved for the French heroine when her sword was finally replaced. The cable TV channels Lifetime Network and History Channel provided $18,000 to fund the restoration. The valorous conqueror, at least for the time being, has returned to her position of power as she continues to cast a protective watch over our nation's capital.

According to Lifetime Network, the Joan of Arc statue is the only female equestrian statue in DC and, according to their count, is one of only 200 historic statues of women in the United States.

SET IN STONE

Why are there nearly 40 stone markers placed around the perimeter of Washington, DC?

Geocachers and history buffs rejoice! Thanks to George Washington and a thorough team of surveyors, individuals can spend their weekends exploring nearly 40 stone markers that helped set the boundary lines of our nation's capital city.

The Residence Act of 1790 granted Washington the authority to select a new capital city for the country. He chose a 100-square-mile site on the Potomac River between the busy ports of Alexandria, Virginia, and Williamsport, Maryland. Appointed by Secretary of State Thomas Jefferson, Major Andrew Ellicott began his initial planning for an approximate survey of the ten-mile square on February 11, 1791. Ellicott hired astronomer and surveyor Benjamin Banneker. Banneker and his survey team began to mark the diamond-shaped boundary of DC by starting at its most southern tip and established the south of the square at Jones Point in Alexandria. A ceremonial stone from 1794 still sits here along the Potomac River, commemorating the starting point of the District's boundary line. Today the large stone is embedded into the seawall of a lighthouse bearing the inscription "The beginning of the Territory of Columbia" on one side. Each of the 40 stones put in place featured the engraving "Jurisdiction of the United States" on one side and "Maryland" or "Virginia" on the other, as well as the year of its placement and distance from the initial stone.

In hopes of protecting the stones, the Daughters of the American Revolution began enclosing them in iron fences. Despite their efforts, many of the stones were either removed, lost, or

---

The Boundary Stones are the oldest federal monuments in the United States.

Left: *DC Boundary Stone Southwest Mile 1, which is the boundary marker one mile NW of the southernmost marker of the original District of Columbia, now in northern Virginia.* Right: *Boundary Stone: Original West Cornerstone. Photos courtesy of zhurnaly (Mark Zimmerman) via Creative Commons.*

buried. Over time, the outline of DC has changed significantly, leaving the stones in unusual locations and in various conditions. Some can be found along sidewalks and in front yards, while others are located in dense forests. Some locations have plaques either attached to the stones or in place of those missing.

BOUNDARY STONES

WHAT: A collection of nearly 40 rocks strategically placed as markers that helped establish the boundary lines of Washington, DC

WHERE: Various locations spread out along the perimeter of Washington's diamond-shaped border

COST: Free

PRO TIP: Boundarystones.org has mapped out each boundary stone's location and displays pictures of each stone, showing them enclosed in iron, concealed behind grates, or visibly set out on display.

GOING TO THE CHAPEL

Where can worshippers go when they're in urgent need of prayer?

From massive conglomerate retailers to drive-thru windows, the twenty-first century continues to be an era characterized by modern convenience. Many of us crave one-stop shops where we can get what we need and get it quickly. So perhaps it should come as no surprise that this full-service concept has transcended the commercial realm and has made its way into places of worship. Those in the DC metro area looking for a quick praying pit-stop are in luck!

Conspicuously tucked along a busy street in Silver Spring, Maryland, there is a tiny chapel that many drivers might whiz right by if they don't know it's there. The compact structure is white, somewhat square-shaped, and about the size of a roadside fruit stand. A short white fence surrounds the building along with a small patch of grass and a few shrubs. There are several lawn chairs outside, a sign reading "Prayer Stop," and three crosses that adorn the front exterior of the building. The mini-chapel seats four; upon entering the church, visitors are greeted by sounds of Christian music.

The Prayer Stop was built in 2000 by a man named Dennis who describes himself as a recovering alcoholic and reformed cheater. After he lost everything, he prayed the Lord's Prayer, cried a bit, and then proceeded to convert a fruit stand into a chapel. The church's creator wanted to provide a place for those in need of prayer

THE PRAYER STOP

WHAT: A compact roadside church where visitors can stop by and pray

WHERE: 16811 New Hampshire Ave., Silver Spring, MD

COST: Free

PRO TIP: Take exit 33B off of I-95 and drive west on Hwy 198/ Sandy Spring Rd. for six miles. Turn right onto Hwy 650/New Hampshire Ave. and drive for almost a mile. The chapel is on the right.

Inside the intimate and tiny Prayer Stop chapel. Photos courtesy of Bohemian Baltimore.

who might otherwise be intimidated by a large church (nearby Immanuel's Church has over 3,000 members). Since its inception, thousands of worshippers from across the country have visited and prayed at the Prayer Stop; many have written messages of hope in the guest book.

The Prayer Stop seats four and features a slot for prayer requests.

BRIDGE TO NOWHERE

Why is there an abandoned and incomplete overpass bridge that leads to nowhere?

Individuals driving along the Clara Barton Parkway near Glen Echo may find themselves wondering why there is a strange overpass that passes under an abandoned, decrepit bridge that seems to lead absolutely nowhere. Why was it built? What master plan was this neglected bridge supposed to be a part of?

In 1930, Congress approved the construction of a parkway lining both sides of the Potomac River. The design outlined two lanes in each direction, extending from Great Falls to Mount Vernon in Virginia and Fort Washington in Maryland. Virginia's highway was completed first. The construction of Maryland's parkway, however, did not go quite as smoothly. The Park Service bought segments of land, as opposed to one continuous stretch, expecting to eventually connect all of the parts. Various groups in Prince George's County, including environmentalists, landowners, and politicians, began to complain that there wasn't a need for a riverfront parkway to link the District to Fort Washington.

The Park Service did proceed to build the parkway north to Glen Echo and beyond; however, there are only two lanes in some places. The overpass bridge, which over time acquired the nickname "the Bridge to Nowhere," was built in hopes of that additional lands would be acquired to complete the parkway. By 1969, it was a foregone conclusion that the Maryland portion of the parkway would never be completed.

The bridge's concrete structure and triple-tiered guardrails correspond with that of the George Washington Memorial Parkway on the opposite side of the Potomac River.

Clara Barton Parkway near Glen Echo, Maryland. Photo courtesy of Famartin via Creative Commons.

It turns out that tearing down bridges, even if they've been deemed completely useless, is just too costly and far more effort than it's worth.

BRIDGE TO NOWHERE

WHAT: An unfinished overpass bridge that's part of a parkway lining the Potomac River

WHERE: Along the Clara Barton Parkway near Glen Echo

COST: Free

PRO TIP: Intrepid visitors will need to conquer the inevitable traffic and carefully climb up and down embankments to reach the dilapidated bridge.

ONE (MAKE THAT 6,800) FOR THE BOOKS AND ONE FATAL NIGHT AT THE THEATRE

Of the numerous memorials honoring President Abraham Lincoln, which one may have been granted the final word?

As one of the most beloved and powerful presidents in US history, there is no shortage of memorials commemorating Abraham Lincoln. From the Lincoln Memorial in Washington, DC to Mount Rushmore in South Dakota, our 16th president has been widely celebrated for well over a century. So, it should come as no surprise that historians have had no choice but to become a bit creative in recent years when honoring the former president.

On President's Day of 2012, a group of historians unveiled a lofty tower of nearly 7,000 books saluting Lincoln's legacy in the middle of a spiral staircase in the lobby of the Petersen House, Ford's Theatre Center for Education and Leadership. The imposing tower measures 34 feet tall and approximately eight feet around. The 6,800 books were assembled from a collection of the nearly 15,000 books that have been written about Lincoln. Other than Jesus Christ, no other individual in history has been written about more than Abraham Lincoln. The enormous conglomeration of books represents a wide range of publications, ranging from scholarly textbooks and

TOWER OF BOOKS

WHAT: A 34-foot-tall tower of 6,800 books honoring President Abraham Lincoln's legacy and the tremendous number of books written about him

WHERE: The Petersen House: 516 10th St. NW, Washington, DC

COST: Visit fords.org/visit/visitor-guidelines for visitor information.

PRO TIP: Visitors can stand in the room where Lincoln died, as well as see several exhibits displaying artifacts from the night of his assassination.

international best sellers to coloring books. Fire marshals need not worry; the impressive tower is solely comprised of aluminum-covered replicas of the books, with the covers of the real books printed on them.

The Petersen House is where Lincoln died after being fatally shot by assassin John Wilkes Booth. On April 14th, 1865, Lincoln attended a performance of *Our American Cousin* at the infamous Ford's Theatre and was shot in the brain by Booth during the show's third act. Booth himself was an actor and had performed at the theatre multiple times before this infamously dreadful night. Deemed too weak to travel back to the White House, Lincoln was transported across the street to the former boarding house, where the owners welcomed a feeble Lincoln into their home. Lincoln died there the next morning at 7:22 a.m. surrounded by his wife, Mary, and various US government officials.

Having been familiar with Ford's Theatre and its layout, John Wilkes Booth was able to meticulously plan his escape route, leaping twelve feet from the presidential box down to the stage, before running out the rear door to nearby Baptist Alley. Booth owned a small stable in the alleyway, jumped upon his bay mare within seconds of exiting the theatre, and galloped away. While unknown to many locals and visitors, Baptist Alley still exists today; its entrance is on F Street NW between 9th and 10th Streets.

OLD CAPITOL PRISON TURNS SUPREME

What previously stood on the US Supreme Court's stomping grounds?

Since its inception in 1789, the US Supreme Court has had a resounding impact on countless aspects of our lives. From public school integration to voting rights, the highest court in the land has been an integral part of the very fabric of our nation. The site of the Supreme Court, however, was not always a place of distinction and justice. In fact, it has quite a long and sordid history.

After the British torched the US Capitol during the War of 1812, Congress built a brick building to serve as a temporary capitol. Once Congress was able to move into its permanent dwelling, the temporary building, now regarded as the Old Capitol, was soon transformed into a boardinghouse. The outbreak of the Civil War, however, left it abandoned and dilapidated. The government removed the fence surrounding the building, replaced the wooden slits above the windows with iron bars, and converted it into a prison.

Many prestigious individuals served prison time here, including Confederate generals, Northern political prisoners, and spies. Many of the spies were women, often playing integral roles

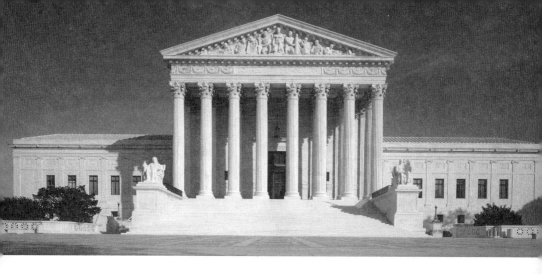

The Supreme Court, the highest court in the land and the former site of the Old Capitol Prison. Photo courtesy of the Collection of the Supreme Court of the United States.

in the Confederate victories. Perhaps the most notable was the beguiling socialite Rose O'Neal, a previous resident of the former boardinghouse turned inmate. O'Neal engaged in spying activities that were pivotal in the Confederate victory at First Bull Run. Rose, along with her daughter, continued to run covert operations while incarcerated for over five months. O'Neal was such a successful spy that Jefferson Davis attributed the victory of the battle of Manassas to her. When she was exiled to the Confederate states after her release from prison, Davis assigned her to lead international missions.

Following the end of the war, in 1867, the prison was sold and turned into rowhouses. In 1929, it was demolished to allow for the construction of the US Supreme Court building, which remains on the site today.

Belle Boyd was another notorious Confederate spy. While imprisoned, she often communicated with outside supporters. Her contact would shoot a rubber ball into her cell so that she could sew messages inside the ball before returning the ball outside her prison window.

HEADS UP: THE CASE OF AN ATTORNEY GENERAL'S MISSING HEAD

How did a prominent US Attorney General's skull end up missing?

Unknown callers and hang-ups can leave many frustrated and perplexed. But imagine receiving a phone call where the caller asks, "Would you be interested in getting William Wirt's head back?" Such was the mysterious call that a Congressional Cemetery manager received in 2003. The manager naturally responded, "yes" before the caller abruptly hung up.

William Wirt served as Attorney General under Presidents James Monroe and John Quincy Adams. Wirt holds the title of longest serving attorney general in United States history, and he is also credited with turning the position into one of national importance. Although Wirt was a prominent figure, when he died in 1834 he left his family in tremendous debt. He was buried in an unmarked grave at Congressional Cemetery. In 1853, Wirt's son-in-law built a massive family vault near the highest point of the cemetery, so large that it remains the biggest and most visible monument on the grounds. Wirt's remains were reinterred in the new family vault with fellow

THE MYSTERY BEHIND ATTORNEY GENERAL WILLIAM WIRT'S MISSING HEAD

WHAT: The mysterious case of Attorney General William Wirt's missing skull, which was stolen from a family vault in the Congressional Cemetery

WHERE: Congressional Cemetery: 1801 E St. SE, Washington, DC

COST: The cemetery is free to explore; tours can be arranged on their website.

PRO TIP: Dog walking is permitted in the cemetery; however, membership is a requirement for dog-walking privileges.

family members, including his wife Elizabeth and daughters Agnes and Ellen.

Following the puzzling 2003 phone call, the cemetery manager decided to probe further. He went out to examine the vault and confirmed that the lock had been removed from of the door and the vault had indeed been vandalized. In place of the lock, a massive slab of granite had been placed in front of the vault's door, simultaneously keeping it closed and blocking its entryway.

After further investigation, it was determined that Robert L. White had collected Wirt's skull, adding to his bizarre collection of 40-some skulls. When White died in 2003, the appraiser of his estate found an old metal box painted with gold block letters reading "Hon. Wm. Wirt." The appraiser ultimately initiated the process of returning the skull to the cemetery. While White is identified as the collector of Wirt's skull, the thief and motive remain a mystery.

It remains unknown when and how the skull was stolen from William Wirt's vault. Robert L. White is believed to have had the skull in his collection for about 18 years before he died. One theory surrounding Wirt's stolen skull was the goal of classifying his intelligence.

I'M A COOL MOM

Where in the Washington, DC, area can you simultaneously shop for groceries while satisfying your arcade game fix?

Washington, DC, may not be a city where people often see eye to eye, but there's one place that parents, kids, foodies, gamers, and *Stranger Things* fans may find that they all have in common. Welcome to MOM's Organic Market in College Park, Maryland, where freshly baked baguettes and artisan cheeses cohabitate with flashing lights, clanging bells, and whirling whistles. Tucked away between the freezers in the frozen foods section next to the bakery lies an arcade nirvana where pinball enthusiasts' dreams come true.

The organic grocery store recently underwent significant renovations and tripled in size, adding a bona fide pinball arcade featuring 29 refurbished machines. A wide array of pop-culture themes is showcased including *Game of Thrones, The Twilight Zone*, AC/DC, and *The Simpsons*. The dedicated pinball parlor comes from the personal collection of MOM'S founder Scott Nash, who has chosen to merge his love for organic produce and gourmet goods with his affinity for pinball machines. The market's arcade section even includes a lounge where friends and relatives of pinball fanatics can sit back, relax, and patiently wait. All of the games cost around 50 cents, and there's a change

MOM'S ORGANIC MARKET PINBALL PARLOR

WHAT: An unusual pinball arcade parlor showcasing 29 pinball machines inside MOM's Organic Market, a grocery store chain in the greater Washington, DC, area

WHERE: MOM's Organic Market: 9821 Rhode Island Ave., College Park, MD

COST: Each of the pinball games cost around 50 cents.

PRO TIP: There are 19 MOM's Organic Market locations. Only the College Park, Maryland, location features a pinball machine parlor.

Get your game on: Pinball machines line MOM's Organic Market's pinball arcade parlor. Photo courtesy of MOM's Organic Market.

machine so that pinball enthusiasts never have to worry about running out of quarters.

A posted sign describes pinball etiquette, including rules about not talking to players or placing food and drinks on top of the machines. The final, and arguably most important, rule reads, "A pinball machine is a work of art, treat it with respect!"

Another sign hanging over the pinball section entrance quotes Dante's *Inferno*, warning gamers to "abandon all hope ye who enter here."

THEY'RE CREEPY AND THEY'RE KOOKY: THE ADAMS MEMORIAL

Which Washington, DC, memorial is shrouded in mystery, despair, and disturbing love and obsession?

Inside Washington, DC's Rock Creek Cemetery sits a creepy, and (according to some) haunted statue of Marian "Clover" Hooper Adams. Hooper Adams was married to Henry Adams, a descendent of John Quincy Adams and John Adams. A prime example of art imitating life, the eerie sculpture is as dismal as the woman it portrays.

Clover Adams was a talented individual praised for her incredible photography, writing, and volunteer work in the Civil War. Sadly, she was often described as unwell, and in 1885, at 42 years old, she committed suicide by swallowing potassium cyanide, a chemical she often used in her photography. Speculation surrounded the motive of her suicide; some thought it was the result of her father's recent death, while others felt it was because her husband was interested in another woman. Henry mourned the loss of his wife, and in many ways the manner in which he grieved was almost as perplexing as his wife's death. He destroyed nearly all of her photographs and letters, and it was said that he never spoke

CLOVER ADAMS MEMORIAL

WHAT: An anonymous and androgynous grave marker memorializing Marian Hooper Adams, an amateur photographer and wife of Henry Adams

WHERE: Section E of Rock Creek Cemetery, Washington, DC

COST: Free

PRO TIP: The Adams Memorial is enclosed by a small circle of trees and marble benches for visitors to sit and be pensive. Its view is typically obstructed.

The mysterious and morbid Adams Memorial. Photo courtesy of the Historic American Buildings Survey.

her name again. Moreover, Henry never even mentioned her in his autobiography, *The Education of Henry Adams*.

The next year, however, after traveling to Japan, Henry commissioned artist Augustus Saint-Gaudens to sculpt a memorial to his late wife. He asked that the Buddhist's philosophy around grief be used to help depict Henry's anguish. The end product was an androgynous and anonymous bronze seated figure enveloped in a garment while casting its eyes downward. Henry was adamant that no name be carved in the sculpture, further perpetuating the mystery surrounding the peculiar couple and Clover's tragic death. The memorial continues to be shrouded in legend, with many claiming ghost sightings and feelings of unease and despair.

There is a replica of the Adams Memorial in the Smithsonian American Art Museum.

ROLL WITH IT: THE PLOTTING OF A PRESIDENTIAL ASSASSINATION

How did a casual Chinatown restaurant become associated with the plotting of a presidential assassination?

Washingtonians and tourists know Wok and Roll, a casual Chinatown eatery, for its Chinese and Japanese fare, along with its happening Karaoke lounge. What many may be surprised to learn is that before the popular restaurant was serving up fried rice and sushi rolls, it was a boarding house where conspirators met and devised an assassination plot that ultimately resulted in President Abraham Lincoln's murder.

In 1853, John Surratt purchased the present-day Wok and Roll building and operated it as a boarding house. Following his death in 1862, his wife Mary Surratt left their Maryland home and moved into the boarding house. From September 1864 to April 1865 during the Civil War, Mary Surratt continued to run the boarding house and welcomed a variety of guests. The most notable and scandalous of all were a group of conspirators who plotted to kidnap and subsequently murder President Abraham Lincoln. Mary met with the team of conspirators, including John Wilkes Booth, at the house, where she supplied Booth and co-conspirator David Herold with guns and field houses. She was later executed by hanging for her role in the plot, becoming the first woman ever executed by the United States federal government.

The building was listed on the US National Register of Historic Places on August 11, 2009.

A HISTORICAL LANDMARK
"SURRATT BOARDING HOUSE"
604 H STREET, N.W. (THEN 541)
IS SAID TO HAVE BEEN WHERE
THE CONSPIRATORS PLOTTED
THE ABDUCTION OF
U.S. PRESIDENT ABRAHAM LINCOLN
IN 1865

PLAQUE BY CHI-AM LIONS CLUB
美京中美獅子分會

Wok and Roll, a popular Chinese restaurant in DC's Chinatown and the location where Abraham Lincoln's assassination was planned. Left photo courtesy of AgnosticPreachersKid via Creative Commons. Right photo courtesy of JoAnn Hill.

Diners and passersby can check out the easy-to-miss plaque that hangs outside of the restaurant commemorating its sordid past.

WOK AND ROLL RESTAURANT

WHAT: A present-day Chinatown restaurant that was once the location of the conspiracy that led to the assassination of President Abraham Lincoln

WHERE: 604 H St. NW, Washington, DC

COST: Dependent on how hungry and thirsty you are

PRO TIP: Wok and Roll Restaurant is a ten-minute walk from Ford's Theater, the infamous site of President Abraham Lincoln's assassination.

AMERICA'S OLDEST APOTHECARY

Where can you visit America's oldest apothecary, complete with its original products?

Long before the Food and Drug Act was enacted and mega-chain pharmacy conglomerates arrived on the healthcare scene, small family-owned apothecaries served as primary sources for medicinal needs. The country's oldest apothecary shop, Stabler-Leadbeater Apothecary, once operated in Alexandria, Virginia. Today the store has been converted into a museum, showcasing its original bottles and instruments and providing a fascinating glimpse into the nearly obsolete apothecary industry.

Following an apprenticeship in Leesburg, Virginia, Edward Stabler opened the Stabler Apothecary in 1792. He developed many of the medicines in the store's upstairs workshop. In addition to selling medicine, Stabler's apothecary carried a wide array of household and outdoor items, including soap, perfumes, farm and garden equipment, dentistry equipment, cigars, paint, brushes, and combs. Stabler's business quickly gained

STABLER-LEADBEATER APOTHECARY MUSEUM

WHAT: A historic apothecary that's been preserved as a museum

WHERE: 105-107 South Fairfax St., Alexandria, VA

COST: Adults: $5.00, Children ages 5-12: $3.00. Children 4 and under are free with a paying adult.

PRO TIP: The museum is 1 mile from the King Street metro. Tours run every half hour at 15 minutes past and 15 minutes before the hour.

Legend has it that Robert E. Lee was in Stabler's Apothecary when he received orders to end John Brown's raid on Harpers Ferry.

Outside of the Stabler-Leadbeater Apothecary Museum. Photo courtesy of Ser Amantio di Nicolao via Creative Commons.

recognition and attracted a wide range of customers. According to sales logs displayed at today's museum, the clientele included several famous historical figures, including Martha and George Washington and Robert E. Lee.

The business stayed within the family, passing from Edward to his son, William, and then to William's brother-in-law John Leadbeater, who added his surname to the business. The apothecary reached its prime in 1865, when it had acquired 11 buildings and warehouses throughout the Washington, DC, region and serviced approximately 500 pharmacies. As times changed, however, the apothecary's success proved to be no match for the emerging synthetic drug companies and the FDA's stringent regulations. The family declared bankruptcy and closed down in 1933. Its historical significance did not go unnoticed, and six years later the apothecary and its products were purchased at an auction by L. Manuel Hendler, an ice cream businessman from Baltimore. The Landmarks Society of Alexandria turned the store into a museum where visitors can view unique artifacts and take an interesting peek into the medicine world's history.

TIME IS OF THE ESSENCE

Where can you find the most important and precise timekeeping device on the planet?

From scheduled meetings and appointments to competitive races and sporting events, our daily lives are often dictated by the universal notion of time. As technology has evolved, the human race has gone from relying on sundials and mechanical clocks to digital clocks and GPS systems. None of these time-tracking devices, however, would be possible without the US Naval Observatory's Master Clock, the most crucial and precise timekeeping system in the world.

Displayed outside of the USNO, the Master Clock is paramount in the determination of exact time and management of time intervals. It's not one clock as the name might suggest, but rather a system of dozens of separate atomic clocks working carefully to count the "swings" of atoms' radiation with an unparalleled level of accuracy. The clocks are dispersed among several buildings across the Observatory's campus and kept under tight security measures. The buildings' temperatures have been strictly regulated to +/- 0.1°C and the humidities controlled to within 3%. Each of the clocks measure time a bit differently according to which ones are being fixed or calibrated at any given moment. Data is derived from a combination of the clocks' measurements. This combination determines the correct time used around the world, from the clocks on our phones, televisions, and computers, to the timekeeping system used by the Department of Defense.

The clocks are not solely based on time, but on space, too. Identifying one's exact place in space depends upon one's exact time at a location. A GPS satellite system consists of 24 satellites;

The US Vice President has lived on the grounds of the 72-acre US Naval Observatory since 1977.

Top: *USNO Master Clock Ensemble.* Inset: *Clocks of the USNO. Photos courtesy of the US Naval Observatory.*

satellites are calibrated daily against the Master Clock. By comparing the time a signal was transmitted by a satellite in space with the time it was received by a GPS receiver on Earth, phones and other devices can determine their distances from each satellite. While the average person probably never even thinks about the Master Clock, it has a tremendous impact on financial, education, and government institutions across the globe.

US NAVAL OBSERVATORY MASTER CLOCK

WHAT: The most precise timekeeping system in the world

WHERE: 3450 Massachusetts Ave. NW, Washington, DC

COST: Free

PRO TIP: While the USNO is closed to the public, visitors can see the Master Clock time digitally displayed outside the front gate.

NOW DIG THIS: HONORING THE AGE OF THE DINOSAURS

What's the meaning behind the dinosaur signs just blocks away from the US Capitol?

While walking or jogging near the Capitol Hill neighborhood's Garfield Park, revered for its sprawling playground, tennis and bocce courts, and picnic area, passersby may find themselves wondering why a street adjacent to the park has been uncharacteristically named Capitalsaurus Court. What could the neighborhood that's most often associated with our seat of government possibly have to do with dinosaurs? Quite a bit, actually.

A single dinosaur vertebra was discovered by workers installing a sewer pipe at 1st and F Streets SE in 1898. Smithsonian Institution researchers designated the found fossil as unique and identified it as a new species nicknamed *Creosaurus potens*, a 30-foot long predator exceeding two and a half tons. Nearly a century later in 1990, local paleontologist Peter Krantz suggested a much snappier name: Capitalsaurus. To celebrate the 100th anniversary of the fossil's uncovering, Krantz worked with local elementary schools to petition the DC Council to name Capitalsaurus as the city's official dinosaur. The Official Dinosaur Designation Act of 1998 was subsequently enacted.

CAPITALSAURUS COURT

WHAT: The Capitol Hill location where a dinosaur fossil was uncovered and that is now regarded as the discovery spot of DC's official dinosaur

WHERE: 1st and F Streets SE, Washington, DC

COST: Free

PRO TIP: In addition to getting its own city block, Capitalsaurus has its own official song, titled "Them Dino Bones."

Capitalsaurus Court displayed proudly on the corner of 1st and F Streets SE. Photos courtesy of JoAnn Hill.

While DC's famed fossil is now housed in the National Museum of Natural History, its original home continues to pay tribute on the city block where it was discovered. A whimsical sign featuring Capitalsaurus chasing a smaller dinosaur, along with a bright green street sign designating this block of F Street SE as Capitalsaurus Court, is prominently displayed.

Since the dinosaur fossil's uncovering, researchers have discovered other fossils from a wide range of years and species in the area, including Virginia's dilophosaurus bones and armored nodasaurs bones in College Park, Maryland.

A MUSHROOM CLUB FOR THE FUN GUY (AND GIRL)

Where can fungi enthusiasts gather to celebrate all things related to mushrooms?

In metropolises like Washington, DC, there is likely a club or group for everyone. Some clubs are more formal and political, like the National Press Club and quasi-secret Chowder and Marching Club, while others focus more around social and active gatherings like kickball and frisbee leagues. What about a club for those who love mushrooms and all things fungi related? No need to worry, because there's a club for that, too! The Mycological Association of Washington (MAW) is the answer for the fun-guy (and girl) who is passionate about the almighty mushroom.

The MAW is a nonprofit organization that originated with the purpose of sharing information and knowledge about fungi. Anyone who has interest in mushrooms is welcome to join to learn and share information about mushrooms, as well as meet other mycophiles. Members range from professional mycologists to beginners. The club meets on the first Tuesday of every month, and meetings are free and open to the public. When attending a meeting, one can expect to hear a brief overview of club news and announcements, identification of mushrooms that members have brought to share with the club, and a guest speaker. Some examples of previous meeting topics include the relationship between mushrooms and plants, truffles and tastings, the use of mushrooms in traditional Chinese medicine, and mushroom photography.

At monthly MAW meetings, if there are mushrooms in the woods, there will be a table of locally harvested mushrooms for members to explore.

Top: Ramaria stricta, *a coral mushroom.*
Inset: Chlorosplenium chloral, *a tiny cup fungus. Photos courtesy of Mark Livezey at Mushroom Observer.*

MYCOLOGICAL ASSOCIATION OF WASHINGTON DC

WHAT: An organization established to share information and knowledge about fungi

WHERE: Meetings are typically held in the basement of Kensington Park Library: 4201 Knowles Ave., Kensington, MD

COST: Membership is free and open to the public.

PRO TIP: Membership is required to attend culinary events. Some forays are members-only, while others charge $5 to non-members.

The MAW offers over a dozen mushroom-hunting forays each year, from morel season in April until the first frost in November. Most forays last between one to four hours and occur in local parks and forests. Some, however, are held outside of the DC area as far away as Front Royal, Virginia, and at Camp Sequanota in south central Pennsylvania, where their annual foray is held.

Of course, no mushroom club is worth its fungi without tasting events. Members who are willing to put forth the effort and time will learn how to distinguish between poisonous and edible mushrooms and can also share mushroom recipes and dishes.

AS WHITE AS A GHOST

Is America's most famous residence also one of the most haunted?

Depending on your political party affiliation, throughout various periods of time, you may find yourself baffled by or even frightened by the individuals occupying the White House. Regardless of your opinion of who's in office, he or she probably is not nearly as terrifying as those who have been known to haunt the residence at 1600 Pennsylvania for centuries after leaving the premises. The most recognizable address in America is also arguably the most haunted, with countless sightings of former presidents, first ladies, and White House staff members.

One of the most frequent ghostly sightings is that of First Lady Abigail Adams. Adams used to hang laundry in the East Room, the warmest and driest room of the White House. Her apparition has been reportedly seen walking toward the East Room dressed in a lace shawl and cap with outstretched arms like she's carrying laundry. President Andrew Jackson has been said to haunt the Rose

GHOST SIGHTINGS AT THE WHITE HOUSE

WHAT: The longtime home of the president of the United States, where ghosts of former presidents, first ladies, and staff members have been sighted

WHERE: 1600 Pennsylvania Ave. NW, Washington, DC

COST: Tours are free and are scheduled on a first come, first served basis.

PRO TIP: The White House is located exactly between two metro stations: McPherson Square Station and Farragut West Station.

Many psychics believe that Lincoln's presence has remained in the White House to serve as an aide during crises as well as to finish the work that was interrupted by his assassination.

Top: *The most famous and recognized house in the United States: The White House. Photo courtesy of Washington.org.* Inset: *The Lincoln Bedroom at the White House. Photo courtesy of Harry S. Truman Library & Museum.*

Room as well as the halls of the president's chambers. The Rose Room served as Jackson's bedroom and is believed by many to be one of the White House's most haunted rooms. Jackson was defeated by John Quincy Adams in one of the most controversial presidential elections in US history. Mary Todd Lincoln, a devout believer of the supernatural, often told friends of hearing Jackson cursing and stomping throughout the halls.

Without a doubt the most persistently reported ghost sighting has been of President Abraham Lincoln. First Lady Grace Coolidge was the first to say that she had seen the 16th president's ghost. According to her account, she saw Lincoln standing near a window in the Oval Office peering across the Potomac River to the former Civil War battlefields. First Lady Eleanor Roosevelt also shared that she often felt Lincoln's presence when working in the Lincoln bedroom. British Prime Minister Winston Churchill recounted a story during one of his stays in the White House of seeing Lincoln sitting by the fireplace in his bedroom. Lady Bird Johnson shared that she felt Lincoln's spirt one night while watching a television feature about his death.

HOFF THE HARMONICA CASE MAN

How did one Washingtonian earn the nickname "Hoff the Harmonica Case Man"?

It's common to acquire new hobbies as we get older. From gardening to golf to crocheting, many of us choose to learn new skills for the mental escape and physical benefits that hobbies often provide. Washingtonian Bob Hoffman did just that and more. After he learned to play the harmonica in his mid-50s, he began collecting unique harmonica cases and ultimately accrued the largest collection of its kind in the world.

What started off as a simple interest soon became a fascinating obsession. Hoffman initially began seeking customized beaded cases that could easily hold and transport his harmonicas in a fashionable manner. This quickly escalated to collecting specially designed cases. Over 15 years later, Hoffman has accumulated more than 500 cases that have been designed by nearly 450 artists. The intricately created cases are made from a variety of materials, including eggshells, glass, plastic, metal, wood, beads, fabric, and ivory. Some of his cases showcase themes or have special meaning, like the ones that have been made by Vermont artisans, paying homage to the spot where Hoffman spends his summers. Other cases prominently display Hoffman's face, ranging from the more serious depictions to the outright outlandish. The nickname "HOFF" is inscribed and appears on every case. A lanyard is attached to each case so that he can wear it around his neck. Each unique case holds the same

Hoffman is always looking for new artisans to design harmonica cases for him. His design guidelines are outlined on his website.

HOFF THE HARMONICA CASE MAN

WHAT: A harmonica-playing man's private collection of harmonica cases, known to be the largest of its kind in the world

WHERE: 1714 North Inglewood St., Arlington, VA

COST: Nothing in Hoffman's collection is for sale

PRO TIP: Hoffman's collection is available to display at gallery shows and exhibitions. His cases and accessories can also be viewed online at: hoffharmonica.com.

size harmonica, which Hoffman purchases in bulk. Hoffman's vast collection of cases contains original work from artists throughout the United States as well as from many artists in countries throughout the world. Hoffman works closely with each artist to co-design each special case.

Hoffman's love for his harmonica collection has extended well past its cases. He has commissioned a number of artists to create harmonica accessories, including jewelry, clothing, hats, posters, and sculptures.

FROM ARSENAL TO ART

What is the history behind how The Torpedo Art Factory Center got its name?

The Torpedo Art Factory Center is often recognized as one of Old Town Alexandria's prized gems. From art studios and galleries to workshops and classes, the sprawling space has something for everyone, regardless of age. It quietly holds the country's largest number of publicly accessible working artists' studios in one collective space. The building, however, wasn't always a creative and vibrant space. Quite the contrary. The Torpedo Art Factory used to be a real-life torpedo factory, where munitions were manufactured for wartime.

On the day following Armistice Day, November 12, 1918, which marked the official end of World War I, the US Navy began construction on the US Naval Torpedo Station. Upon completion, the station was responsible for the production and maintenance of Mark III torpedoes for the next five years. Manufacturing stopped in 1923, and the space was then transformed into a storage space for munitions until 1937, when the Mark XIV torpedo began being built to be used in World War II. This torpedo was painted green so that the Navy could locate it in the water when it was tested at Piney Point, Maryland. At the conclusion of World War II in 1945, the weaponry plant continued to produce parts for rocket engines before closing permanently in 1946.

Following its 30-year run as an armaments producer, the complex was converted into the Federal Records Center, where it

---

Transforming the former torpedo plant into an art center was originally pitched by the chair of the Alexandria Bicentennial Commission as a three-year pilot. Emerging as a nationally recognized art complex was never part of the plan.

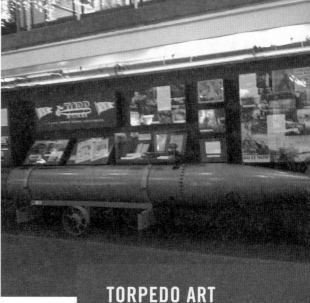

Left: *Exterior view of the Torpedo Art Factory Center in Alexandria, VA. Photo courtesy of Ad Meskens via Creative Commons.* Right: *The green Mark XIV torpedo prominently displayed in the art center's main hall. Photo courtesy of Brownpau via Creative Commons.*

TORPEDO ART FACTORY CENTER

WHAT: A naval munitions factory that was converted into a popular art center

WHERE: 105 N. Union St., Alexandria, VA

COST: A wide array of art classes and workshops are available for children and adults. Visit theartleague.org/classes for more information

PRO TIP: Today the Mark XIV green torpedo is prominently displayed in the art center's main hall.

stored a myriad of government items, including congressional documents, dinosaur bones belonging to the Smithsonian, and Nuremberg War Crimes trial records. In 1969, the City of Alexandria purchased the building, and a year later the Art League took over the space, transforming the arms plant into artisan studios. Today more than 165 artists work, exhibit, and sell their art spread throughout the complex's three floors. The expansive space houses 82 studios, two workshops, and seven galleries. Visitors are encouraged to watch and interact with sculptors, painters, jewelry makers, photographers, and other artists working with other expressive art modalities.

SITTING PRETTY: THE BEST SEAT IN THE NEIGHBORHOOD

What's the story behind the colossal seat situated in the middle of an Anacostia intersection?

Washington, DC, is the epitome of the expression "Go big or go home." It is a metropolis often defined by its enormity: huge government, monumental memorials, and immense power. It turns out a gigantic chair can also be added to DC's long list of historical, recognizable, and sizeable landmarks.

Looming over the intersection of Martin Luther King Avenue and V Street in the southeast neighborhood of Anacostia, the colossal chair is hard to miss, and it has become an area icon. Its inception dates back to 1959, when Bassett Furniture Industries created the African Mahogany chair for a local company called the Curtis Bros. Furniture Company. The chair served as a new and innovative model of advertising. Coming in at an impressive 19.5 feet tall and a hefty 4,600 pounds, it was identified as the largest chair in the world.

However, that recognition wasn't enough for Bassett. They thought the chair would be even more compelling if they had an individual living on top of the chair inside a glass cube. They hired a glassmaker to build a glass home, complete with curtains along with a bed, shower, toilet, and television. The cube also had three transparent sides, allowing passersby to see its occupant. Next, they searched for a person willing to live inside. Rebecca Kirby, a

THE BIG CHAIR

WHAT: An enormous chair that has become a historic landmark in the Anacostia neighborhood

WHERE: 1001–1199 V St. SE, Washington, DC

COST: Free

PRO TIP: The chair replica is no longer made of wood but rather aluminum, designed to stand the test of time.

Top: *Restaurants and shops line the streets of DC's Anacostia neighborhood.* Inset: *A landmark in its own right: The famous and hard-to-miss Big Chair. Photos courtesy of Washington.org.*

19-year-old model, who went by the name Lynn Arnold, was up to the task, and on August 13, 1960, a forklift raised her up. Advertisements called her "Alice in the Looking-Glass House." Kirby stayed in the cube for 42 days, before it became too taxing and she decided to come back down. She was compensated approximately $1,500 and became a legend in DC advertising.

Today, a replica of the famed chair prominently towers over the same intersection, having replaced the deteriorating original back in 2005.

While the Big Chair once reigned as the world's tallest chair, it has lost its title to various chairs around the globe, including a 56-foot rocking chair in Illinois and a 98.5-foot bright red chair in Austria.

THE MIXED-UP FILES OF THE UNDERGROUND

How did the country's most respected cemetery become shrouded in controversy and cover-ups?

Sometimes even the most revered and esteemed institutions are susceptible to hiccups. As in, mammoth, centuries-lasting, hard-to-rebound-from hiccups. Arlington Cemetery, the country's most important burial ground, is no exception. In 2010, the famous resting place, which occupies approximately 624 acres overlooking the capital city, was rocked by a scandal of lies, mismanagement, and corruption.

After an extensive investigation, it was determined that thousands of graves had been mismarked and some graves had more than one body buried in them. Management was uncooperative during the investigation, even after multiple family members complained that new grave markers had arrived where their kin was laid to rest. The investigation revealed that nearly half of all the files from recent years had either been lost or misplaced, and millions of dollars had been inappropriately expended, as some shady outside contractors had been paid twice for the same job.

When bodies were disinterred to ensure that the correct soldier was in the correct grave, the investigation confirmed that many soldiers had been haphazardly and dishonorably buried. When investigators examined the paperwork for three sections of

---

The Tomb of the Unknown Soldier, a memorial to the casualties of World War I, World War II, the Korean War, and the Vietnam War, is guarded by sentinels from the 3rd US Infantry Regiment 24 hours a day, every day of the year, in any weather.

Arlington Cemetery: The country's most important burial ground. Photo courtesy of Arlington National Cemetery.

SCANDAL AT ARLINGTON CEMETERY

WHAT: A colossal scandal involving mismarked graves and multiple bodies being buried under one headstone at the United States' most important cemetery

WHERE: Arlington National Cemetery, Arlington, VA

COST: Free

PRO TIP: As many as 25 to 30 funeral services occur each day, excluding Sundays and federal holidays, 9 a.m. to 3 p.m. on weekdays and 9 a.m. to 2 p.m. on Saturdays.

the cemetery, they discovered that over 200 headstones did not match the soldiers buried underneath. Those shady contractors were still maintaining records as they did in the late 1800s, scribbling burial information on tiny scraps of paper that would eventually be either lost or destroyed. Some soldiers were accidentally buried on top of one another and then later exhumed without family members being notified. It turns out that families of thousands of dead American soldiers may have been mourning at the wrong graves for years.

GRAB YOUR RUBBER DUCKIE: BATH TIME AT THE SENATE

Why are two mysterious bathtubs housed in the US Capitol basement?

It should come as no surprise that the general public isn't always privy to the daily discussions and decisions made behind the closed doors of the United States Capitol. Individuals may, however, be surprised that secrets of the iconic legislative entity run much deeper than hush-hush lobbying, and questionable policy making. On August 17, 1936, workers discovered two large, marble, and incredibly dusty bathtubs down in the Capitol's underground chamber.

The tubs were installed in the late 19th century. As renovations of the Capitol Building neared completion in 1858, a senator approached one of the engineers with a somewhat unusual request: he wanted to have six bathtubs placed in the basement. At the time, during the months Congress was in session most senators lived in boarding houses that typically lacked indoor plumbing. The senator's request was granted, and six large, Italian marble tubs were planted in the Capitol's basement. Two years later, they

One of two abandoned bathtubs that sits in the basement of the US Capitol. Photo courtesy of Brian Purdy.

were in full use, soon becoming a highly sought-after destination for politicians looking for a place to relax, fraternize, and write and rehearse important speeches. Senators would sometimes invite guests, as soaking in a spacious tub was widely considered a rare and luxurious treat.

As times changed indoor plumbing became more and more readily available, so the previously in-demand tubs lost their mass appeal. By 1890, four of the six tubs were removed, leaving just two tubs to serve as remnants of simpler and more primitive times. Visitors fortunate to be guests of Capitol Hill staff can gain access to the boiler room, where the two remaining tubs are housed. While the tubs have become obsolete, security guards do continue to use the running water, only now for toilets.

Each of the six bathtubs measured three by seven feet and were carved by hand in Italy. When they were installed, the tubs were divided equally: three on the House side and three on the Senate side.

A WAKE-UP CALL: A TRIBUTE TO WOMEN

What inspired the transformation of defunct callboxes into female-focused art installations?

For centuries, history books, monuments, and memorials have overwhelmingly cast a spotlight on male figures. From Franklin Delano Roosevelt to General Philip Sheridan, men, particularly white men, have dominated the capital region's esteemed monument collection. Out of some 160 monuments and memorials in the capital region, just over 50 statues include women. A local artist and an ambitious project answered the call to change that.

The DowntownDC Business Improvement District and the DC Commission on Arts and Humanities partnered with artist Charles Bergen to reimagine nine nonfunctioning call boxes as public art installations. Throughout the 19th century, cast-iron call boxes served as an early emergency alert system predating telephones and two-way radio systems. These call boxes are still scattered across the city, but they haven't been in operation since the 1970s. Bergen worked with urban historian Mara Cherkasky to identify a number of prominent women throughout history for the project. The list included Civil Rights activist Mary Church Terrell, *Washington Post*

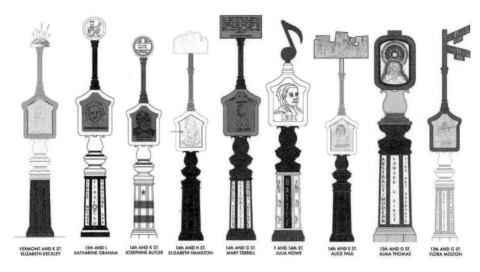

The nine callboxes honoring famous women in US history. Image courtesy of Charles Bergen.

publisher Katharine Graham, Gospel street musician Flora Molton, DC Statehood Party activist Josephine Butler, expressionist painter Alma Thomas, author Julia Ward Howe, National Woman's Party leader Alice Paul, Elizabeth Keckley, a confidante of Mary Todd Lincoln, and Elizabeth Schuyler Hamilton, founder of a New York orphanage. Each callbox includes a sculpture inside, usually with a painted metal symbol that represents the woman's contribution (a guitar for Molton, for example), and dates of birth and death.

The locations of the female-focused callboxes are: Mary Church Terrell (14th and G St. NW), Katherine Graham (15th and L St. NW), Flora Molton (13th and G St. NW), Josephine Butler (14th and K St. NW), Alma Thomas (13th and G St. NW), Julia Ward Howe (14th and F St. NW), Alice Paul (14th St. and Pennsylvania Ave. NW), Elizabeth Hobbs Keckley (Vermont and K St. NW), and Elizabeth Schuyler Hamilton (14th and H St. NW).

In addition to the aforementioned nine women depicted in the callbox refurbishment project, other famous individuals have also been featured, including Prince, whose callbox is located in Capitol Hill.

SOLID AS A ROCK

Why is there an abandoned large pile of rocks left deep within Rock Creek Park?

Rock Creek Park, Washington DC's popular urban park, provides an oasis for countless outdoor and fitness enthusiasts, as well as those seeking a reprieve from the hustle and bustle of urban living and perpetual grind of DC politics. It also serves as the home of a surprisingly historical and important mound of rocks.

While the US Capitol was undergoing renovation in 1958, the project's chief architect removed hundreds of blocks from the building; some were indistinct slabs, while others were embellished carved pieces. Most were part of the monument's original construction. Because the law prohibited the selling or discarding of these historic stones, the builders, not entirely sure where to dispose of them, discreetly deposited them behind a maintenance shed in Rock Creek Park. For over 60 years, this colossal pile of rocks has remained abandoned and virtually untouched.

Advisory architects had suggested donating the stones to the Smithsonian, but Congressman William Steward from Delaware had deemed sandstone to be "deficient" and lobbied hard for the stones to be put out of sight, out of mind.

Piling On: The Capitol Stones hidden deep in Rock Creek Park. Photo courtesy of Ben Swenson.

Today these nearly hidden mammoth stones are covered in moss. The heaps of stones, some nearly 20 feet tall, are arranged in what appear to be orderly rows. Each stone has its own unique features; some are intricately carved, while others have cornices jutting out. These historical stones are entirely abandoned; as neither the US Capitol nor National Park Service has claimed ownership or chosen to maintain the neglected site. While the path leading up to the stones is unmarked, it is essentially clear and easy to navigate.

THE RELIGIOUS ROAD TO THE WHITE HOUSE

Why on heaven's earth are there nearly 50 religious institutions on one particular road leading to the White House?

Sixteenth Street NW is a main thoroughfare that runs through the heart of downtown DC. Spanning nearly 6.5 miles from the White House to the Maryland border, the busy street is lined with beautiful greenery, charming rowhouses, and a staggering number of religious institutions. From grand churches and synagogues, to intricately designed temples and shrines, a wide array of religions is prominently represented along this road. So, just how did one singular street acquire nearly 50 houses of worship?

When Pierre L'Enfant designed the city, he modelled 16th Street after the wide-open boulevards seen throughout much of Europe, offering a majestic view of the White House. For centuries, the imposing street's desirable location and prestigious reputation has attracted esteemed institutions and businesses. In 1816, the street's first church, St. John's Episcopal Church, opened its doors; others of its kind quickly followed suit. Shortly thereafter, Mary Foote Henderson, known as "The Empress of 16th Street," and

---

Many of the institutions on 16th Street have become more diverse over time. Chua Giac Hoang Vietnamese Buddhist Temple became the first Vietnamese Buddhist temple on the East Coast when it was founded in 1976. Saint Stephen and the Incarnation Episcopal Church was the first integrated Episcopal Church in DC, and Shrine of the Sacred Heart now holds mass in four different languages.

Left: *Church of Jesus Christ of Latter Day Saints. Photo courtesy of Farragutful via Creative Commons.* Center: *Shrine of the Sacred Heart. Photo courtesy of Farragutful via Creative Commons.* Right: *St. John's Episcopal Church. Photo courtesy of Kurt Kaiser.*

her senator husband, moved into the neighborhood and began to take command over developing the region. During the late 1800s, the elite couple had purchased a considerable amount of real estate along 16th Street and methodically sold it off to individuals wanting to build mansions, embassies and churches. By the 1920s, Mary had sold two substantial areas of land to the Mormons and the Unitarians. The houses of worship they built along 16th Street remain there today. Simultaneously, zoning laws began prohibiting commercial businesses on 16th Street, creating more space for additional religious institutions to move into.

SIXTEENTH STREET'S NEARLY 50 HOUSES OF WORSHIP

WHAT: An extensive stretch of nearly 50 churches, temples, synagogues, and shrines along Washington's 16th Street NW

WHERE: 16th Street NW, Washington, DC

COST: Free and open to all.

PRO TIP: St. John's Episcopal Church has been attended by every president since James Madison.

Even with the large number of holy places on 16th Street, as time passed, so have some of the buildings' contents. Central Presbyterian, for example, has been converted into a public charter school, while Meridian Hill Baptist has been transformed into a high-end apartment complex. Despite evolving times, the "Avenue of the Churches," as it's been often dubbed, remains the city's epicenter of holiness, making some ponder: Does the road to heaven actually run through the White House?

SAVE A SEAT FOR SCIENCE

Which DC monument encourages visitors to sit and climb upon its statue?

Many of the capital city's monuments ask visitors to quietly reflect when visiting, creating tranquil and sometimes even somber memorial site settings. One lesser-known monument, however, has chosen to take a quite different approach; visitors coming to pay tribute to one of the world's most famous scientists are encouraged not only to sit on his statue, but also to climb upon it.

Standing twelve feet tall and weighing approximately four tons, a bronze statue honoring physicist Albert Einstein is situated near the southwest corner of the National Academy of Sciences (NAS) grounds. In 1979, the NAS unveiled the sizable statue to commemorate the centennial of Einstein's birthday. The famous physicist appears relaxed, leisurely sitting on a three-step bench made of white granite. The figure's left hand holds a paper with mathematical equations showcasing three of his most important scientific contributions: the photoelectric effect, the theory of general relativity, and the equivalence of energy and matter. The statue's base is characterized by a star map—a 28-foot expanse of emerald pearl granite that's embellished with more than 2,700 metal studs representing the sun, moon, stars, planets, and other astronomical objects precisely placed by astronomers from the US Naval Observatory as they were on the centennial date.

ALBERT EINSTEIN BRONZE STATUE

WHAT: A monumental bronze statue honoring physicist Albert Einstein

WHERE: 2101 Constitution Ave. NW, Washington, DC

COST: Free

PRO TIP: Legend has it that if you rub Einstein's nose, some of his genius will rub off on you.

Children climb on top the massive bronze statue honoring physicist Albert Einstein. Photo courtesy of Washington.org.

The German-born scientist was inducted into the NAS in 1922, a year after he won the Nobel Prize in physics. At the time, only US citizens could be elected as full members, so he entered as a "Foreign Associate." In 1940 he became a US citizen, and two years later he was inducted as a full member, serving until his death in 1955.

If you stand directly in the center of the statue, look directly at Albert Einstein, and speak, you will hear a distinct echo.

OOPS! WE DIDN'T MEAN TO SHOOT, MR. PRESIDENT!

Why was the Lincoln Memorial fired upon by the US Army?

The Lincoln Memorial is a national treasure, commemorating one of America's most revered presidents, Abraham Lincoln. Adorned with 36 columns, one for each state in the Union at the time Lincoln died, it is one of the country's most iconic and cherished memorials. The colossal monument is linked to many momentous occasions throughout history, including serving as the location of Martin Luther King, Jr.'s "I have a dream" speech. What many may be surprised to learn is that nearly 80 years ago, it was also the site of an accidental shooting by the US Army.

In 1942, as part of World War II defenses, an anti-aircraft gun was installed atop the US Department of Interior. The gun was positioned near a local bridge to protect the city against an air attack. On September 3, at 10:00 a.m. in the morning, a US Army soldier accidentally released a round of ammunition at the Lincoln Memorial. The accidental firing left its mark on the east side of the memorial. Bullets struck the structure's frieze and damaged three of the 36 states' names: Connecticut, Maryland, and Texas.

US ARMY FIRING UPON THE LINCOLN MEMORIAL

WHAT: An accidental firing upon the Lincoln Memorial during World War II by the US Army

WHERE: 2 Lincoln Memorial Circle NW, Washington, DC

COST: Free

PRO TIP: The north wall contains a typo from Lincoln's second inaugural address. The word "FUTURE" is misspelled as "EUTURE," an error that remains visible today.

Sitting tall: The colossal statue of President Abraham Lincoln. Photo courtesy of Washington.org.

It is certainly safe to say that the Lincoln Memorial is one of very few US buildings that came under attack during World War II. It's even safer to say that it may just be the one structure that was attacked by its own country.

A baseball-size indentation was imprinted into the marble of the memorial's outer wall. The gouge has been fixed before, but the patchwork has fallen out. There are no plans to refill or fix the hole.

SOURCES

Jefferson Memorial: Leave Those Dancing Shoes at Home: Mathis, Sommer. "Woman Arrested for Dancing at the Jefferson Memorial." dcist.com, April 14, 2018. https://dcist. com/story/08/04/14/woman-arrested; "Jefferson Memorial Flash Mob Arrested for Dancing, Protesting Court Ruling." huffpost.com, May 30, 2011. https://www.huffpost. com/entry/jefferson-memorial-dancing-arrests_n_868719.

Discord and Discoloration at the US Capitol: Free Tours by Foot Tour; "The Shooting of Congressman William Taulbee on the Steps of the U.S. Capitol." U.S. House of Representatives History, Art, and Archives website, February 28, 1890. https://history. house.gov/Historical-Highlights/1851-1900/The-death-of-Congressman-William-Taulbee- on-the-steps-of-the-U-S--Capitol.

Stairway to Creepiness: "The Exorcist Stairs." Atlas Obscura. https://www.atlasobscura. com/places/the-exorcist-stairs-washington-dc; Krishnamoorthy, Aparna. "The Exorcist Steps, D.C.'s Most Frightfully Famous Staircase." cutluretrip.com, May 23, 2017. https:// theculturetrip.com/north-america/usa/washington-dc/articles/the-exorcist-steps-d-c-s- most-frightfully-famous-staircase.

I Got You, Babe: "Sonny Bono Memorial Park." Atlas Obscura. https://www.atlasobscura. com/places/sonny-bono-memorial-park; Blitz, Matt. "How DC Ended Up with a Park Dedicated to Sonny Bono." Washingtonian.com, July 31, 2015. https://www. washingtonian.com/2015/07/31/sonny-bono-park-dc-geary-simon.

Name That Tune: The Metro Edition: Interview with Jason Mendelson; Aratani, Lori. "This Guy Wrote a Song for Every Metro Station. All 91 of them." Washingtonpost.com, June 12, 2017. https://www.washingtonpost.com/local/trafficandcommuting/this-guy- wrotea-song-for-every-metro-station-all-91-of-them/2017/06/12/6cbf345a-4acb-11e7- 9669-250d0b15f83b_story.html.

One Man's Trash Is Another Man's Masterpiece: "The Throne of the Third Heaven of the Nations' Millennium General Assembly." Smithsonian American Art Museum website. https://americanart.si.edu/artwork/throne-third-heaven-nations-millennium-general- assembly-9897; Church, Jason. "James Hampton's Throne of the Third Heaven of the Nations' Millennium General Assembly." National Center for Preservation Technology and Training website, June 16, 2015. https://www.ncptt.nps.gov/blog/james-hamptons- throne-of-the-third-heaven-of-the-nations-millennium-general-assembly.

J, Jay, or I: The Real Reason Why There Is No J Street: Johnson, Matt. "Washington's Systemic Streets." Greater Greater Washington website, August 7, 2009. By Matt Johnson. https://ggwash.org/view/2530/washingtonssystemic-streets; "Why is there No J Street in DC? Blame Latin." Ghosts of DC website, January 30, 2013. https://ghostsofdc. org/2013/01/30/why-is-there-no-j-street.

A Fairyland to Call Home: "National Park Cemetery." Alexander Company website. https:// alexandercompany.com/projects/national-park-seminary; "National Park Cemetery." Atlas Obscura. https://www.atlasobscura.com/places/national-park-seminary.

First Lady Séance at the Soldiers' Home: Interview with historian and author Tim Krepp; Mast, Erin Carlson. "Mary Lincoln's Séance at the Soldiers' Home." Lincoln Cottage website, October 30, 2009. https://www.lincolncottage.org/mary-lincolns-seance-at-the- soldiers-home; "The Spiritualist Who Warned Lincoln Was Also Booth's Drinking Buddy." Alford, Terry. Smithsonian Magazine, March 2015. https://www.smithsonianmag.com/ history/the-spiritualist-who-warned-lincoln-was-also-booths-drinking-buddy-180954317.

Taking a Stand: U.S. National Arboretum – "Discover" https://www.usna.usda.gov/discover/gardens-collections/national-capitol-columns/. "National Capitol Columns." Atlas Obscura. https://www.atlasobscura.com/places/washington-mini-monument.

Abused and Abandoned: The Demise of the Forest Haven Asylum: Maurer, Pablo Iglesias. "Abandoned D.C.: Inside the Ruins of the Forest Haven Asylum." dcist.com, November 18, 2014. https://dcist.com/story/13/11/18/abandoneddc-haven; Knipfer, Cody. "Exploring the Forest Haven Asylum: A Hopeless Home for Abandoned People." reallycoolblog.com, January 3, 2019. www.reallycoolblog.com/exploring-the-forest-haven-asylum-a-hopelesshome-for-abandoned-people.

Built on a Bordello and the Oldest Profession in the World: Capitol Hill Scandals Tour, Free Tours by Foot DC; "Confederate Spy Belle Boyd is Captured." History.com, November 13, 2009. https://www.history.com/this-day-in-history/confederate-spy-belleboyd-is-captured; "Old Capitol Prisoner War Camp." mycivilwar.com. https://www.mycivilwar.com/pow/dc-old-capitol.html.

Huddle Up: A Sign of the Times: "Home of the Huddle." gallaudetathletics.com. https://www.gallaudetathletics.com/sports/fball/homeofthehuddle; Okrent, Arika. "The True Origin Story of the Football Huddle." theweek.com, February 2, 2014. https://theweek.com/articles/451763/true-origin-story-football-huddle.

Micro Showcase & Five Signs: Small Sizes, Big Regrets: Onsite Visit, https://microshowcase.com.

The Pentagon and the Illuminati: Siddiqui, Faiz. "15 Potential Illuminati Headquarters Around the World." the complex.com, April 18, 2013. https://www.complex.com/popculture/2013/04/potential-illuminati-headquarters-around-the-world/the-pentagon; Merron, Jeff. "9 Amazing Facts about the Pentagon." mentalfloss.com, November 2, 2016. http://mentalfloss.com/article/87527/9-amazing-facts-about-pentagon.

Foamhenge: Not Your Environmentalist's Monument: Interview with Foamhenge artist Mark Cline; "Foamhenge." roadsideamerica.com. https://www.roadsideamerica.com/story/9209; "Foamhenge: Exact Replica of the Ancient Monument, but Much Lighter." Atlas Obscura. https://www.atlasobscura.com/places/foamhenge.

Living in a DC Barbie World: Leshan, Bruce. "DC's 'Barbie Pond': Quirky, Irreverent, and Maybe Profound." wusa9.com, November 16, 2018. https://www.wusa9.com/article/news/local/dc/dcs-barbie-pond-quirky-irreverent-and-maybe-profound/65-615344674; Plott, Elena. "What's Really Going on with Barbie Pond on Avenue Q?" Washingtonian.com. September 15, 2016. https://www.washingtonian.com/2016/09/15/the-barbie-pond-on-avenue-q-whats-really-going-on-here.

Keep It in the Vault: Voigt, Morgan. "10 Facts You May Not Know about Congressional Cemetery." dcist.com, December 18, 2019. https://dcist.com/story/19/12/18/10-facts-you-may-not-know-about-congressional-cemetery; "The Public Vault." Congressional Cemetery website. https://congressionalcemetery.org/2018/07/25/the-public-vault.

Seeing Double: A Hidden Mini Replica: "Washington Mini Monument." Atlas Obscura. https://www.atlasobscura.com/places/washington-mini-monument.

You Can Lead a Man to Water: Onsite Visit; Carter, Elliot. "Temperance Fountain." July 21, 2016. https://architectofthecapital.org/posts/2016/7/21/temperance-fountain.

Finally, On the Mark: Capitol Hill Scandals Tour, Free Tours by Foot DC; Lefrak, Mikaela. "President Garfield Was Shot on the National Mall. The Site Only Just Got a Plaque." wamu.org, November 18, 2018. https://wamu.org/story/18/11/20/president-garfield-was-shot-on-the-national-mall-the-site-only-just-got-a-plaque.

Ask and Say Yes: "Booth #6—Martin's Tavern." Martin's Tavern website. https://www.martinstavern.com/history/; Heil, Emily. "JFK's Proposal to Jackie at Martin's Tavern Is Legend No More." washingtonpost.com, June 23, 2015. https://www.washingtonpost.com/news/reliable-source/wp/2015/06/23/jfks-proposal-to-jackie-at-martins-tavern-is-legend-no-more.

Sorry for Stealing, but Please Tighten Your Security: Schweitzer, Allie. "The Art of the Steal: A Brief History of Museum Theft in D.C." washingtoncitypaper.com January 15, 2014. https://www.washingtoncitypaper.com/arts/museums-galleries/blog/13080204/the-art-ofthe-steal-a-brief-history-of-museum-theft-in-d-c; "Was Stolen Statue Lesson in Security?" Beaver County Times, January 14, 1983. https://news.google.com/newspapers?nid=2002&dat=19830114&id=ct4qAAAAIBAJ&sjid=stoFAAAAIBAJ&pg=4543,2481461.

A Whole Lotta Junk: The Vanadu Art House: Interview with Vanadu Art House artist and owner Clarke Bedford; Dvorak, Petula. "Suburban Burning Man: a Weird, Art-Encrusted Cottage on an Ordinary Street." washingtonpost.com, March 25, 2019. https://www.washingtonpost.com/local/suburban-burning-man-a-weirdart-encrusted-cottage-on-an-ordinary-street/2019/03/25/c630e8a8-4efc-11e9-88a1-ed346f0ec94f_story.html

The Plane! The Plane!: "Gravelly Point Park." Atlas Obscura. https://www.atlasobscura.com/places/gravellypoint-park; "Gravelly Point Park." https://www.virginia.org/listings/OutdoorsAndSports/GravellyPoint.

A Grave Situation: How Robert E. Lee's Garden Became a Graveyard: "History of Arlington Cemetery." Arlington National Cemetery website. https://www.arlingtoncemetery.mil/Explore/History-of-Arlington-National-Cemetery; Poole, Robert M. "How Arlington Cemetery Came to Be." Smithsonian Magazine Online, November 2009. https://www.smithsonianmag.com/history/how-arlington-national-cemetery-came-to-be-145147007.

One Tough Tree: Calfas, Jennifer. "Bonsai tree, nearly 400 years old, survived Hiroshima and is still flourishing in D.C." usatoday.com, August 5, 2016. https://www.usatoday.com/story/news/nation/2015/08/05/bonsai-tree-nearly-400-years-old-survived-hiroshima-and-stillflourishing-dc/31164857; Nodjimbadem, Katie. "The 390-Year-Old Tree That Survived the Bombing of Hiroshima." Smithsonian Magazine Online, August 4, 2015. https://www.smithsonianmag.com/history/390-year-old-tree-survived-bombing-hiroshima-180956157.

What Lies Beneath: Onsite Tour; Ayres, Kayelynn. "Adventures in DCLand: Brookland's Underground Catacombs." ourcommunitynow.com, January 11, 2019. https://ourcommunitynow.com/attractions/adventures-in-dcland-brooklands-undergroundcatacombs; Franciscan Monastery of the Holy Land in America website, https://myfranciscan.org/visit.

Eat, Sleep, Spy: Espionage at the Mayflower Hotel: DiLiegro, Allison. "Inside the Covert Affairs: Scandal, and Spies at the Mayflower Hotel in Washington DC." https://storiedhotels.com/washington-dc-hotels/inside-the-covert-affairs-scandal-and-spies-at-the mayflowerhotel-in-washington-dc; Wallace, Robert and H. Keith Melton. "Spies, Spies Everywhere: Journey through D.C. Espionage." washingtonpost.com, February 17, 2017. https://www.washingtonpost.com/graphics/lifestyle/washington-dc-spy-map.

Where Fallen Ships Are Laid to Rest: "The Ghost Fleet of Mallows Bay." Atlas Obscura. https://www.atlasobscura.com/places/the-ghost-fleet-of-mallows-bay-nanjemoymaryland; Strochlic, Nina. "'Ghost Fleet' of Sunken Warships Declared a National Marine Sanctuary." nationalgeographic.com, July 8, 2019. https://www.nationalgeographic.com/culture/2019/07/ghost-fleet-sunken-warships-declared-national-marine-sanctuary.

Hannibal Lecter Has Met His Match: "Alferd Packer Cannibal Plaque." Atlas Obscura. https://www.atlasobscura.com/places/alferd-packer-memorial-grill-plaque; "Alferd Packer: Notorious Cannibal." Colorado Virtual Library. https://www.coloradovirtuallibrary.org/digital-colorado/colorado-histories/beginnings/alferd-packer-notorious-cannibal.

Digging, Bigamy, and Compulsion in the Underground: "Were Tunnels Dug Just for Fun or Something More Sinister?" deseret.com, October 21, 1992. https://www.deseret.com/1992/10/21/19011739/were-tunnels-dug-just-for-fun-or-something-more-sinister; Smith, Ryan P. "The Bizarre Tale of the Tunnels, Trysts, and Taxa of a Smithsonian Entomologist." Smithsonian Magazine Online, May 13, 2016. https://www.smithsonianmag.com/smithsonian-institution/bizarre-tale-tunnels-trysts-and-taxa-smithsonian-entomologist-180959089/

Cheers to That! Onsite Visit; Rhodes, Jesse. "The Rickey Declared D.C.'s Native Cocktail." Smithsonian Magazine Online, July 19, 2011. https://www.smithsonianmag.com/arts-culture/therickey-declared-dcs-native-cocktail-32599822/; Carmen, Tim. "The Rickey Earns a Place in D.C. History." washingtonpost.com, July 15, 2011. https://www.washingtonpost.com/blogs/all-we-can-eat/post/the-rickey-earns-a-place-in-dc-history/2011/07/14/gIQAFE6MGI_blog.html

Beyond the Grave: The Mystery behind Jane Doe's Identity: "The Grave of the Female Stranger."Atlas Obscura. https://www.atlasobscura.com/places/the-grave-of-the-female-strangeralexandria-virginia; Mello-Klein, Cody. "The Mystery of the Female Stranger." alextimes.com, August 31, 2019. https://alextimes.com/2019/10/female-stranger.

Ghosted in Daniels: Goran, David. "After It Was Flooded in 1972, The Ghost Town of Daniels Lives as a Collection of Memories." thevintagenews.com, June 21, 2016. https://www.thevintagenews.com/2016/06/21/flooded-1972-ghost-town-daniels-lives-collectionmemories/; "Visiting Maryland's Ghost Town: Daniels." midatlanticdaytrips.com, October 18, 2015. http://www.midatlanticdaytrips.com/2015/10/visiting-marylands-ghost-town-daniels.html.

Signed, Sealed, but Thankfully Not Delivered: Kelly, John. "A Strange Bit of DC Lore: Were Two Hobos Almost Entombed in a Memorial? Washingtonpost.com, January 21, 2015. https://www.washingtonpost.com/local/a-strange-bit-of-dc-lore-were-two-hobos-almostentombed-in-a-memorial/2015/01/21/b91f4daa-a193-11e4-9f89-561284a573f8_story.html; Maura. "The 10 Weirdest and Strangest Things That Have Ever Happened in Washington, DC." Onlyinyourstate.com, November 12, 2016. https://www.onlyinyourstate.com/dc/weirdest-things-washington-dc/

Round and Round: A Carousel Takes a Turn into the Civil Rights Movement: "How a Carousel Ride Became Part of America's Civil Rights History." pbs.org, August 26, 2013. https://www.pbs.org/newshour/arts/entertainment-july-dec13-carousel_08-26; Hinton, Tristiana. "The Carousel on The Mall: Spinning Civil Rights History." wtop.com, February 26, 2012. https://wtop.com/news/2012/02/the-carousel-on-the-mall-spinning-civil-rights-history.

The Dog Days of the US Postal System: "Owney, Mascot of the Railway Mail Service." National Postal Museum. https://postalmuseum.si.edu/exhibits/current/moving-the-mail/mail-by-rail/owneymascot-of-the-railway-mail-service/all-about-owney/index.html; Childs, Arcynta Ali. "Owney The Mail Dog." Smithsonian Magazine Online, September 2011. https://www.smithsonianmag.com/arts-culture/owney-the-mail-dog-48862403.

Calling All Stomachs of Steel: National Museum of Health and Medicine website. https://www.medicalmuseum.mil; Perrottet, Toni. "The National Museum of Health and Medicine." Smithsonian Magazine Online, June 2011. https://www.smithsonianmag.com/arts-culture/the-national-museum-of-health-and-medicine-161045363.

Bald-Headed and a Little Bit of Comfort: Edwards, Owen. "Kilroy Was Here." Smithsonian Magazine Online, October 2004. https://www.smithsonianmag.com/history/kilroy-washere-180861140/; Soniak, Mat. "What's the Origin of 'Kilroy Was Here'?" mentalfloss.com, June 19, 2013. https://www.mentalfloss.com/article/51249/whats-origin-kilroy-was-here.

To the Moon and Back: "The Space Window at National Cathedral in Washington." Washington National Cathedral website. https://cathedral.org/cathedral-age/the-space-window; "The 'Space Window'" NASA website, September 10, 2012. https://www.nasa.gov/topics/history/features/spacewindowhistory.html; King, Kristi. "Where to Find Rock from Apollo 11 Moon Mission at DC's National Cathedral." wtop.com, July 10, 2019. https://wtop.com/gallery/media-galleries/where-to-find-rock-from-apollo-11-moon-mission-at-dcs-national-cathedral.

Sprucing Things Up with Some Chainsaw Sculptures: "Glenwood Cemetery's Chainsaw Structures." Atlas Obscura. https://www.atlasobscura.com/places/glenwood-cemeterys-chainsawsculptures; "Wooden Sculptures in Glenwood Cemetery." dcbikeblogger. wordpress.com, August 8, 2014. https://dcbikeblogger.wordpress.com/2014/08/08/wooden-sculptures-in-glenwood-cemetery.

The Mushroom House: Kashino, Marisa M. "Bethesda's Famous 'Mushroom House' Is for Sale." Washingtonian.com, May 16, 2018. https://www.washingtonian.com/2018/05/16/bethesdas-famous-mushroom-house-is-for-sale/; Sergent, Jennifer. "The Mushroom House: Before and After." May 27, 2018. https://jennifersergent.com/real-estate/the-mushroom-house-before-and-after.

Hindu Goddess and President Barack Obama: Ghouse, Mike. "Goddess Saraswati Statue with Barack Obama Symbolizes Relationship between Indonesia and the U.S." huffpost.com, December 6, 2017. https://www.huffpost.com/entry/goddess-saraswati-statue-_b_3460615?guccounter=1&guce_referrer=aHR0cHM6Ly93d3cuZ29vZ2xlLmNvbS88&guce_referrer_sig=AQAAAA7IW4C4JHL_I9LzMIsNjhDmIP1jWPO4VGCFlvX8uitKVA3CYLJ9rBW_K2SjWNMweQT2-bVT4nR2--BsqHvFFx1ZDHhxpi0Rv6sLHJTbh06YZzNidhEoAkDH4pwIDu0JhjKmGbamWMNGjdg7YDE9q91UBqR0shiRTL9_0mN397WN; "Indonesia Gifts U.S. a Saraswati Statue." thehindu.com, June 10, 2013. https://www.thehindu.com/news/international/world/indonesia-gifts-us-a-saraswati-statue/article4798380.ece.

Raising Cane: Free Tours by Foot Tour; "Canefight! Preston Brooks and Charles Sumner." ushistory.org. https://www.ushistory.org/us/31e.asp; "The Caning of Senator Charles Sumner." US Senate website. https://www.senate.gov/artandhistory/history/minute/The_Caning_of_Senator_Charles_Sumner.htm#:~:text=On%20May%2022%2C%201856%2C%20the,beat%20a%20senator%20into%20unconsciousness.

On the Straight and Narrow, in Spite of It All: Bailey, Steve. "A Tiny, Beloved Home That Was Built for Spite." nytimes.com, February 29, 2008. https://www.nytimes.com/2008/02/29/travel/escapes/29away.html; Alex. "Which of Old Town Alexandria's Spite Houses Is Narrowest? It's a Game of Inches!" oldtownhome.com, February 23, 2018. https://www.oldtownhome.com/2018/2/23/Which-of-Old-Town-Alexandrias-Spite-Houses-is-Narrowest-Its-a-Game-of-Inches

When Three and a Half Minutes Feels Like an Eternity: "Wheaton Station Metro." Atlas Obscura. https://www.atlasobscura.com/places/wheaton-station-escalator.

The Truth Shall Set You Freely Talking: "St. Elizabeths Hospital." Atlas Obscura. https://www.atlasobscura.com/places/st-elizabeths.

A Penny for Your Thoughts: Actually, Make That 10,000: Onsite Interview; Le Dem, Gaspard. "This Eckington Couple Made a D.C. Map out of 10000 Pennies in Their Shower." dcist.com, August 19, 2019. https://dcist.com/story/19/08/19/this-eckington-couple-made-a-d-c-map-out-of-10000-pennies-in-their-shower,

A Spy and a Soviet Walk into a Bar: "Aldrich Ames." FBI website. https://www.fbi.gov/history/famous-cases/aldrich-ames; Devaney, Robert. "Spies Like Us: The Spooks of Georgetown." Georgetowner.com, October 24, 2019. https://georgetowner.com/articles/2019/10/24/spies-like-us-the-spooks-of-georgetown.

Art Imitates Life and Go-Go Plays On: Uliano, Dick. "Chuck Brown Day: DC Celebrates Beloved Musician." wtop.com, August 18, 2018. https://wtop.com/dc/2018/08/chuck-brown-daydc-celebrates-beloved-go-go-musician/; Ramanathan, Lavanya. "Chuck Brown Memorial Park Honors D.C.'s Go-Go Godfather." washingtonpost.com, April 21, 2014. https://www.washingtonpost.com/news/going-out-guide/wp/2014/08/21/chuck-brown-memorial-park-honors-d-c-s-go-go-godfather.

The Apple Doesn't Fall Far from the Tree: "NIST Newton Apple Tree." Atlas Obscura. https://www.atlasobscura.com/places/nist-newton-apple-tree.

Pet Cemetery: A Final Burial Place for Beloved Pets: Interview; Blitz, Matt. "55,000 Pets—And 30 People—Are Buried in Silver Spring's Aspin Hill Memorial Park." Washingtonian.com, December 11, 2015. https://www.washingtonian.com/2015/12/11/55000-petsand-30-peopleare-buried-in-silver-springs-aspin-hill-memorial-park.

The World's Most Dangerous Hot Dog Stand: Interview with tour guide and historian Tamara Belden; Smith, Steven Donald. "Pentagon Hot Dog Stand, Cold War Legend, to Be Torn Down." US Department of Defense website, September 20, 2006. https://archive.defense.gov/news/newsarticle.aspx?id=1049; Stilwell, Blake. "Why the Soviet Union Wanted to Nuke This Hot Dog Stand," wearethemighty.com, February 15, 2019. https://www.wearethemighty.com/history/ussr-nuke-hot-dog-stand?rebelltitem=1#rebelltitem1

Under His Eye: Kelly, John. "A Creepy Mannequin Stares Down from an Alexandria Apartment Building. Why?" washingtonpost.com, March 23, 2019. https://www.washingtonpost.com/local/a-creepy-mannequin-stares-down-from-an-alexandria-apartment-buildingwhy/2019/03/23/58e5d14c-4b40-11e9-9663-00ac73f49662_story.html; "He's Been Watching: The Looming Sentinel of Old Town." alextimes.com, February 11, 2007. https://alextimes.com/2011/02/hes-been-watching-the-looming-sentinel.

Prost! A Brewmaster and His Castle: Padua, Pat. "Inside the Brewmaster's Castle." dcist.com, November 30, 2011. https://dcist.com/story/11/11/30/gallery-inside-the-brewmasterscast/;https://heurichhouse.org/learn.

Oh, Say Can You Cheat: An Affair Turns Deadly: Veroske, Ariel. "Cold-Blooded Murder in Lafayette Square: The Sickles Tragedy of 1859." boundarystones.weta.org, June 24, 2013. https://boundarystones.weta.org/2013/06/24/cold-blooded-murder-lafayette-squaresickles-tragedy-1859; Young, Greg. "Insanity: 160 Years Ago Today, Congressman Daniel Sickles Shot and Killed the Son of Francis Scott Key." boweryboyshistory.com, February 27, 2019. https://www.boweryboyshistory.com/2019/02/insanity-160-years-ago-todaycongressman-daniel-sickles-shot-and-killed-the-son-of-francis-scott-key.html.

Enchantment in a Storybook Forest: Interview; Kaltenbach, Chris. "A Look at the Enchanted Forest in Ellicott City through the Years." Baltimoresun.com, October 9, 2017. https://www.baltimoresun.com/features/retrobaltimore/bal-through-the-years-the-enchanted-forest-20171005-photogallery.html; http://www.clarklandfarm.com/enchanted_forest.html.

We're Waiting for You, Madam President: Boissoneault, Lorraine. "The Suffragist Statue Trapped in a Broom Closet for 75 Years." Smithsonian Magazine Online, May 12, 2017. https://www.smithsonianmag.com/history/suffragist-statue-trapped-broom-closet-75-years-180963274/;"Women in Art" https://www.aoc.gov/women-art.

A Sword and Its Sorcerers: Heggpeth, Dana. "How Will This Joan of Arc Defeat Her Enemies? Sword Goes Missing from Statue in D.C. Park." washingtonpost.com, September 22, 2016. https://www.washingtonpost.com/local/public-safety/somethings-missing-from-a-dc-park-the-sword-from-joan-of-arcs-statue/2016/09/22/d92e56f2-80c8-11e6-a52d-9a865a0ed0d4_story.html; Cartagena, Rosa. "People Have Been Stealing the Sword from this Joan of Arc Statue." Washingtonian.com, November 30, 2016. https://www.washingtonian.com/2016/11/30/people-have-been-stealing-the-sword-from-this-joan-of-arc-statuemeridian-hill-park-for-over-80-years.

Set in Stone: "Boundary Stones of the District of Columbia." https://www.boundarystones.org/; "Find the Stones that Mark the Original Boundary of the District of Columbia." National Parks Service website. https://www.nps.gov/experiences/dc-boundary-stones.htm

Going to the Chapel: "People from All Over Visit Silver Spring Prayer Stop." wusa9.com, April 19, 2017. https://www.wusa9.com/article/news/local/people-from-all-over-visit-silverspring-prayer-stop/432568955; https://www.roadsideamerica.com/tip/13631.

Bridge to Nowhere: "D.C.'s 'Bridge to Nowhere.'" washingtonpost.com, September 10, 2011. By John Kelly. https://www.washingtonpost.com/local/dcs-bridge-to-nowhere/2011/08/25/gIQA2QiPIK_story.html.

One (Make That 6,800) for the Books and One Fatal Night at the Theatre: "34-Foot-Tall Tower of 6,800 Fake Lincoln Books" https://www.roadsideamerica.com/story/36090; "Baptist Alley" https://www.atlasobscura.com/places/baptistalley; https://www.fords.org/visit/historic-site/petersen-house/Ford's Theatre; Onsite tour

Old Capitol Prison Turns Supreme: Free Tours by Foot Tour; "Confederate Spy Rose O'Neal Greenhow Dies." history.com, November 13, 2019. https://www.history.com/this-day-in-history/rose-greenhow-dies.

Heads Up: The Case of an Attorney General's Missing Head: Grabowski, Mark W., Douglas W. Owsley, and Karin S. Bruwelheide. "Cemetery Vandalism: The Strange Case of William Wirt." *Washington History* 22 (2010): 57–68. https://www.jstor.org/stable/41000589?seq=1; Interview with historian and author Tim Krepp; Brammer, Robert. "'Would You Be Interested in Getting (Attorney General) William Wirt's Head Back?' Rebecca Roberts Brings Us a Tale from the Congressional Cemetery." Library of Congress website, August 14, 2017. https://blogs.loc.gov/law/2017/08/would-you-be-interested-in-getting-attorneygeneral-william-wirts-head-back-rebecca-roberts-brings-us-a-tale-from-the-congressionalcemetery.

I'm a Cool MOM: Beckwith, Alison. "Inside the New Mom's Organic Pinball Arcade." hyattsvillewire.com, July 8, 2018. https://www.hyattsvillewire.com/2018/07/08/moms-organicmarket-pinball-arcade/; "Pinball Parlor at MOM's Organic Market." Atlas Obscura. https://www.atlasobscura.com/places/pinball-parlor-at-moms-organic-market.

They're Creepy and They're Kooky: The Adams Memorial: "Adams Memorial." Smithsonian American Art Museum website. https://americanart.si.edu/artwork/adams-memorial-21528; "Clover Adams' Memorial: From a Husband Who Would No Longer Speak Her Name." Atlas Obscura. https://www.atlasobscura.com/articles/adams-memorial-rock-creek-cemetery-washington-dc.

Roll with It: The Plotting of a Presidential Assassination: Interview with historian and author Tim Krepp; "Lincoln's Assassination Was Planned at This D.C. Karaoke Spot." pbs.org, April 14, 2015. https://www.pbs.org/newshour/nation/lincolns-assassination-planned-d-c-karaoke-spot; "Mary Surratt Boarding House Is Now a Chinese Restaurant." ghostsofdc.org, March 2, 2015. https://ghostsofdc.org/2015/03/02/mary-surratt-house-wok-roll-dc,

America's Oldest Apothecary: "The Apothecary Museum." alexandriava.gov, March 28, 2018. https://www.alexandriava.gov/historic/apothecary/default.aspx?id=36978; "Stabler- Leadbeater Apothecary Museum." Atlas Obscura. https://www.atlasobscura.com/places/stabler-leadbeater-apothecary-museum.

Time Is of the Essence: Pasternak, Alex. "How the Master Clock Sets Time for The World." vice.com, November 6, 2014. https://www.vice.com/en_us/article/3dkd5b/demetriosmatsakis-and-the-master-clock; "USNO Master Clock." https://www.usno.navy.mil/USNO/time/master-clock.

Now Dig This: Honoring the Age of the Dinosaurs: Black, Riley. "'Capitalsaurus,' A D.C. Dinosaur." Smithsonian Magazine Online, September 28, 2010. https://www.smithsonianmag.com/science-nature/capitalsaurus-a-dc-dinosaur-90370223; Gaynor, Michael J. "Happy Capitalsaurus Day!" washingtonian.com, January 25, 2013. https://www.washingtonian.com/2013/01/25/happy-capitalsaurus-day-1.

A Mushroom Club for the Fun Guy (and Girl): Mycological Association of Washington, DC, website. http://www.mawdc.org.

As White as a Ghost: "Ghosts in the White House." history.com, August 12, 2019. https://www.history.com/topics/halloween/ghosts-in-the-white-house; "The Haunted White House." American Hauntings. https://www.americanhauntingsink.com/haunted-white-house.

Hoff the Harmonica Case Man: Onsite Interview; James, Megan. "An Afternoon with Hoff and the World's Largest Harmonica-Case Collection." sevendaysvt.com, September 4, 2013. https://www.sevendaysvt.com/vermont/an-afternoon-with-hoff-and-the-worlds-largestharmonica-case-collection/Content?oid=2265924; https://www.hoffharmonica.com/internationalcases.

From Arsenal to Art: Kelly, John. "An Art Center Now, Alexandria's Torpedo Factory." Washingtonpost.com, August 30, 2014. https://www.washingtonpost.com/local/an-art-center-now-alexandrias-torpedofactory-began-life-making-weapons/2014/08/30/31a55ec0-2e0f-11e4-994d-202962a9150c_story.html; Torpedo Factory Art Center website. http://torpedofactory.org/about-us/history.

Sitting Pretty: The Best Seat in the Neighborhood: Muller, John. "Anacostia Larger-Than-Life Big Chair Is Full of Neighborhood History." ggwash.org, March 27, 2015. https://ggwash.org/view/37647/anacostias-larger-than-life-big-chair-is-fullof-neighborhood-history; Koslof, Evan. "Why Is There a Big Chair in Anacostia?" wusa9.com, December 19, 2018. https://www.wusa9.com/article/news/local/dc/why-is-there-a-big-chair-in-anacostia/65-624082535.

The Mixed-Up Files of the Underground: Benjamin, Kathy. "The Scandalous History of Arlington National Cemetery." mentalfloss.com, May 27, 2012. https://www.mentalfloss.com/article/30776/scandalous-history-arlington-national-cemetery; MacAskill, Ewen. "US Outrage as Scandal Grows Over Arlington Military Grave Mix-up." theguardian.com, July 29, 2010. https://www.theguardian.com/world/2010/jul/29/us-arlington-military-headstones-mixup.

Grab Your Rubber Duckie: Bath Time at the Senate: Interview with historian and author Tim Krepp; Robinson, Emily. "The Congressional Bathtubs." blogs.weta.org, January 24, 2018. https://blogs.weta.org/boundarystones/2018/01/24/congressional-bathtubs; "Mystery of the Senate Bathtubs." US Senate website. https://www.senate.gov/artandhistory/history/minute/Mystery_of_the_Senate_Bath_Tubs.htm.

A Wake-Up Call: A Tribute to Women: Lefrak, Mikaela. "Historic Downtown Call Boxes Are Now Mini-Museums to Famous Women." npr.org, October 16, 2019. https://www.npr.org/local/305/2019/10/16/770688172/historic-downtown-call-boxes-are-now-minimuseums-to-famous-women; Lefrak, Mikaela. "Historic Call Boxes in Downtown D.C. Will Be Transformed into Art Celebrating Women." wamu.org, November 9, 2018. https://wamu.org/story/18/11/09/historic-call-boxes-in-downtown-d-c-will-betransformed-into-art-celebrating-women

Solid as a Rock: Carter, Elliot. "Capitol Stones in Rock Creek Park." architectofthecapitol.com, September 5, 2016. https://architectofthecapital.org/posts/2016/5/30/capitol-stones; Blitz, Matt. "The Historic Capitol Stones Are Hidden in Plain Sight." Washingtonian.com, August 7, 2015. https://www.washingtonian.com/2015/08/07/the-historic-capitol-stones-are-hidden-in-plain-sight.

The Religious Road to the White House: "Dozens of Houses of Worship Line 16th Street NW. Here's Why." Dcist.com, August 16, 2017. https://dcist.com/story/17/08/16/houses-of-worship-16th-st; Lefrak, Mikaela. "Why Are There Nearly 50 Houses of Worship on 16th Street in D.C.?" npr.org, October 1, 2019. https://www.npr.org/local/305/2019/10/01/765841389/why-are-there-nearly-50-houses-of-worship-on-16th-street-in-d-c.

Save a Seat for Science: "Albert Einstein Bronze Statue." Atlas Obscura. https://www.atlasobscura.com/places/albert-einstein-bronze-statue; "NAS Building: Albert Einstein Memorial" National Academy of Sciences website. http://www.nasonline.org/about-nas/visiting-nas/nas-building/the-einstein-memorial.html.

Oops! We Didn't Mean to Shoot, Mr. President! Ebner, Tim. "The Absolute Weirdest Things That Had Ever Happened in Washington DC." Thrillist.com, December 14, 2015. https://www.thrillist.com/lifestyle/washington-dc/8-of-the-weirdest-thingsto-ever-happen-in-washington-dc; King,Kristi. "A Rare Birds-eye View from the Top of the Lincoln Memorial." wtop.com, June 14, 2018. https://wtop.com/local/2018/06.

INDEX